M000227147

"Sensuous, compassionate, and utterly unflinching." — **Jane Hirshfield**

"A monumental achievement." — **D. Nurkse**

"High art, a mystical enchantment." — **Rafael Jesús González**, First Poet Laureate of Berkeley CA, Professor Emeritus Creative Writing & Literature and Mexican Studies, Laney College

"It is difficult to resist the temptation to compare Mary Mackey to Elizabeth Bishop." — *The Huffington Post*

"Mary Mackey is a national treasure." — *Tulsa Book Review*

"*Creativity: Where Poems Begin* is a remarkable book in which Mary Mackey charts the paths of her own creativity as she tries to discover an entry point to the magical place where the seed of a poem starts to open. . . She finds within herself the ability to enter a trancelike state beyond words that she can visit again and again, pen in hand, open to possibility and ready to bring the unfolding beauty and mystery of poetry back into the ordinary world." — **Lucille Lang Day**, author of *Birds of San Pancho and Other Poems of Place*

"In this brilliantly written, profound, and deeply personal account of how creative ideas have come to her, Mary Mackey takes us on a journey to the place where poetry begins. Her quest makes *Creativity* a book for anyone who wants to understand how bursts of insight come not only to poets and writers, but to all of us." — **Mara Lynn Keller**, PhD, Professor Emerita of Philosophy and Religion and Women's Studies, California Institute of Integral Studies

"Mary Mackey is a brilliant feminist explorer seeking the source of the poetic Nile, creating a ... book—part personal (how she became a poet, featuring a treasure trove of poems) and part universal (a guide to unlocking and accessing creativity). I love this book. I'll forever be savoring the nuggets of wisdom found in these pages." — **Richard Peabody**, editor, *Gargoyle Magazine*

"Mackey is a magnificent thinker with broad passions. ... Her work, while stunningly layered, is always accessible." — **CompulsiveReader.com**

ALSO BY
Mary Mackey

Poetry

The Jaguars That Prowl Our Dreams (March Hawk Press)
Travelers With No Ticket Home (Marsh Hawk Press)
Sugar Zone (Marsh Hawk Press)
Breaking The Fever (Marsh Hawk Press)
The Dear Dance of Eros (Fjord Press)
Skin Deep (Gallimaufry Press)
One Night Stand (Effie's Press)
Split Ends (Ariel Press)

Novels

The Village of Bones (Lowenstein Associates)
The Widow's War (Berkley Books)
The Notorious Mrs. Winston (Berkley Books)
The Year The Horses Came (Harper San Francisco)
The Horses at the Gate (Harper San Francisco)
The Fires of Spring (Penguin)
Season of Shadows (Bantam)
The Kindness of Strangers (Simon & Schuster)
A Grand Passion (Simon & Schuster)
The Last Warrior Queen (Putnam)
McCarthy's List (Doubleday)
Immersion (Shameless Hussy Press)

Novels Published
Under The Name "Kate Clemens"

Sweet Revenge (Kensington Books)
The Stand In (Kensington Books)

Creativity

Where Poems Begin

Mary Mackey

MARSH HAWK PRESS

East Rockaway, New York • 2022

Copyright © 2022 by Mary Mackey

All rights reserved.

ISBN: 978-1-7326141-2-3

No part of this book may be reproduced or used in any form or by any means, electronic or mechanical, including photocopying, recording, or by any information storage and retrieval system, without permission in writing from the publisher, unless faithfully conforming to fair use guidelines.

Marsh Hawk books are published by Marsh Hawk Press, Inc., a not-for-profit corporation under section 501(c)3 United States Internal Revenue Code.

Publication of this title was made possible in part by a regrant awarded
and administered by the Community of Literary Magazines and Presses (CLMP).
CLMP's NYS regrant programs are made possible by the New York State Council on
the Arts with the support of Governor Kathy Hochul and the New York State Legislature.

Front cover photograph: Susan Quasha
Back cover photograph: Mary Mackey, Costa Rica, 1968
Book design: Susan Quasha

FIRST EDITION

Library of Congress Cataloging-in-Publication Data

Mackey, Mary, author.
Creativity : where poems begin / by Mary Mackey.
First edition. | East Rockaway : Marsh Hawk, 2022]
LCCN 2021061256 | ISBN 9781732614123 (paperback)
LCSH: Mackey, Mary. | Poets, American—20th century—Biography. |
   Creation (Literary, artistic, etc.) | Poetry—Authorship. | LCGFT: Autobiographies.
LCC PS3563.A3165 Z46 2022 | DDC 811/.54 [B—dc23/eng/20211222
LC record available at https://lccn.loc.gov/2021061256

Marsh Hawk Press
P.O. Box 206, East Rockaway, N.Y. 11518-0206
www.marshhawkpress.org

For A.W.

Contents

INTRODUCTION

What Is Creativity?

What is creativity? Where do creative ideas come from? What happens at the exact moment a creative impulse is suddenly transformed into something that can be expressed in words?

To describe creativity is extraordinarily difficult, because the moment of creation comes from a place where language does not exist and where the categories that determine what we see, hear, taste, and feel are not immediately present.

In our daily lives we tend to live on the surface, unaware of the complexity and richness of what lies below. Poetry creates itself, bubbling up from the depths until it reaches that part of our brains that transforms consciousness into words. Like music, a poem can be understood in a dozen different ways, all interacting with one another. This means a poem can form a continuous bridge between the moment of creation and its incarnation in language.

Poems can also be taken apart line by line, metaphor by metaphor and held up for rigorous, logical inspection; but when this happens, there is always something essential missing. For this reason, almost every chapter in this book begins and ends with a poem that illustrates and often comments on its contents, enfolding and enriching the prose with elements that the prose alone cannot express.

Poetry chose me; I did not choose it. Call it an involuntary act of creation, a constantly surprising connection between self and non-self, a movement from seen to unseen and back again. Call it at its best moments the movement of an adult mind back to the radical innocence and vision of the very young child who sees, not only the reality we all share, but all those unnamed, unclassified parts of reality we learn to overlook as we grow older.

This book is a journey to the place where poems begin. I invite you to join me.

—M.M.

1

Words

Nothing of my birth. No memory of the womb, the darkness, the warmth. But there is a low hiss that comes to me in dreams like the flow of a great river, and a rhythm—a sound—something that pulses in me for the rest of my life: controlling my tongue, the measure of my thoughts, the timing of my heart.

My memories go back a long way, too long to be true, people tell me. And yet they are there, stored in a wordless space in my mind, because they came before words, existing in a place that someday I will come to understand is the source of my poetry, perhaps the source of all poetry. It is a country without borders, a place without language, a universe that has not yet been talked into being.

For an infinite period, I rest outside of time. There are colors, forms, sounds, smells, but they sweep through me undifferentiated and unrecorded. Every moment is new. Nothing makes sense, but this does not bother me, because I have no expectation that it should. I feel pleasure but do not grasp at joy, because I have no sense that joy is finite. I feel pain but do not fear suffering, because I do not yet know that pain can persist, grow worse, or return.

I float in the material world as I floated in my mother's womb: conscious and unconscious at the same time. I float in infinity, and it is beautiful. What a pathetic word to describe such greatness. "Beautiful?" Say rather "ecstatic," and even that does not begin to capture the bliss of it.

Slowly, my parents and the other humans who surround me talk me into reality like people welcoming a child to live in a great mansion if she will only abandon all that exists outside its walls. Their words are the stones, their emotions and gestures the mortar that will seal me off from wordless infinity.

Yet I need to live in the world of other humans, the world of time, the world of words. Something in me craves this, grasps for it; and as I seize their words, suck on them, unfold them inside myself and let the long tendrils of their sounds attach to objects, that fragment of the whole that we humans have all agreed to call 'reality' begins to congeal around me. And this is where my real memories begin, sharp and defined, and undeniably experienced; because later I check them out with my parents and find that they remember the same things:

A wooden crib, slick with yellow varnish. Two teddy bears painted on the panel at my feet: one wearing a pink dress, one wearing a blue one. Wooden bars that look like the naked trunks of trees. A cream-colored enamel saucepan with a red stripe around the rim attached to a broom handle and stuck out the window to catch snow which is mixed with sugar and vanilla. A small child's table with a square hole in the middle where I am placed to eat.

What do these things have to do with anything? What do a crib, a table, and a saucepan have to do with becoming a poet?

The answer is: everything. These objects are not important in themselves. They are only crucial because I remember them by name. This marks a momentous divide. At this moment, I am still poised between a wordless infinity and the sharply defined, limited, and absolutely necessary world of common human experience and culture that recognizes, among other things, cause and effect, time, reason, and death. This is a transitional moment, a moment when I have acquired my first words—priceless tools, which will allow me to communicate with other human beings and, to a limited extent, with animals.

As I sit at that child's table eating sugared snow cream, I am still capable of sensing the infinite wordless space of my infancy, and at the same time, because I have words, I can remember that timeless floating well enough to attempt to describe it to you. At the age of two, I am in touch with a boundless source of inspiration, and I have language. In other words, I have everything I will need to become a poet except education and experience.

And words. I will need many more words before I actually begin to write, because ultimately words are what will make me into a poet instead of, say, a painter or a musician.

Words will become my tools and my most treasured possessions. I love them from the very first. I fall on them the way other children fall on candy. I beg my mother and father to tell me what things are called, and my parents, who believe a rich vocabulary is one of the best gifts parents can give a child, are happy to comply.

"Say 'hippopotamus,'" my father urges, as he teaches me my first multisyllabic word. "Here is a picture of one. They live far away in a place called 'Africa.'"

"Don't say: 'Can I have a popsicle,'" my mother tells me. "Say 'May I have a popsicle.' 'Can' means you are asking if it is possible to have one. 'May' means you are asking my permission."

It is estimated that there are one million distinct words in the English language. At the age of two, I probably know 150 to 200. By the time I am three, I know something in the range of 1,000 to 1,500 words and can use them more or less in context. I don't understand everything my parents are telling me, but without realizing it, I have begun to assemble my poetic toolbox. I talk to myself, to my stuffed animals, to trees, rocks, birds, cups, and other people; and in doing so, I learn that I have a talent for remembering and reproducing sounds. I can order them properly. I have a general grasp of what they mean.

Almost immediately, I start playing with words like toys, combining and recombining them. I ask my teddy bear: "Can a hippopotamus have a popsicle? No. Popsicles are too cold. Can a popsicle have a hippopotamus?"

I imagine a popsicle eating a hippopotamus. *Cherry,* I think. *A cherry popsicle with a big red mouth. Hard to chew on a hippopotamus. This popsicle needs teeth.*

I go on spinning out that idea, and in the process, I discover something important: In an English sentence, when you turn the order of the words around, they sometimes create a world different from the one you live in.

I find this highly entertaining. I can do it for hours at a time. I invent an imaginary friend and invite her to join me, my teddy bear, and the imaginary hippopotamus-eating popsicle for a tea party. I hear a recording of "Frere Jacques" in English and French, and begin to make up "French" words, not having any idea what a foreign language is and not realizing that multiple speakers have to agree on what a word means, and that not just any old sound will do.

I am only a small child who cannot yet read, but in an incomplete, awkward way I have produced my first poems, because the essence of poetry and of imagination itself involves playing with language, inventing new combinations, turning things on their heads, and defying expectations.

I make mistakes. I forget. I pronounce words improperly and am corrected, primarily by my mother for whom proper pronunciation and grammar are Articles of Faith in a religion that falls just a notch below Methodism. I welcome her corrections. I persist in loving words, and my vocabulary grows rapidly. By the time I am an adult and have been writing, reading, and studying for more than half a century, I will possess an English vocabulary of more than 60,000 words and a considerably more modest vocabulary in several foreign languages. And I will have become a poet.

Words made this possible. Words turned me into a writer, but with each word I acquired, I lost something vital, something important that most of us are taught to abandon at a very early age.

When, for example, I learned the word "chair," I came to see tens of thousands of objects as "chairs" no matter how different they were from one another. In essence, when I acquired language, I entered a world of categories and abstractions and stopped actually seeing what was in front of me. This was, of course, necessary. If I had preserved an awareness of all the individual details of the world—every shift in light, every whorl in wood, every leaf and stone and grain of sand—I would have been incapable of action.

I needed a filter that would allow me to focus primarily on things important to my own survival. I needed to be aware of cars speeding toward me when I crossed the street and not be distracted by oil making rainbow patterns in puddles. I needed to be able to recognize other people even when they had lost weight or cut their hair. Most of all, I needed to become oblivious of and unresponsive to the immense amounts of sense data that constantly competed for my attention.

My brain, restructured to a large extent by the language and the culture into which I was born, became that filter. Freed from a constant bombardment of information, I embraced an attenuated consciousness of reality and became a normal, sane adult human being. The price I paid for this was to become blind to much of what surrounded me. But I was not blind all the time, because as I grew to adulthood, I retained a partial ability to stand on the threshold that marks the boundary between childhood and adulthood and see and not see at the same time.

When I write a poem, my mind continues to move fluidly between the real and the surreal. I experience ordinary, plain, unadorned reality; and at the same time, I see the alternatives that reality offers, the dream-like possibilities that cluster around objects, the barely-conscious connections between words, images, scents, sounds, and touch. I can look at a bowl sitting on a table and see it simply as a white china bowl; but at the same time I can see it—as I have written in my poem "The Breakfast Nook"—as "a white sound/ swirling into a depression/ of unspeakable depths." I can pick up a fork and see it simply as a fork, which is what I do most of the time, because to do anything else would be impractical when I am eating. But if I concentrate on that fork, focus unwavering attention on it, I can see it as a "long shining road/that branches at the end/into four paths/that lead nowhere."

I don't drink alcohol or take drugs to enter this state of mind. It comes as naturally as breathing. All I need to do is shift my attention and look at something as if I have never seen it before. The world we have agreed to call "the surreal" is hidden in plain sight. It always clusters around the real the way the petals cluster around the central disk of a sunflower. I can choose to ignore the surreal, ignore the real, or use both in a poem. But I don't create either. They just exist simultaneously.

Which brings me back to words. Valuable as they are, words, by their very nature, aren't good at describing the wordless state. But of all word forms, poetry—spoken, sung, or written—comes the closest, and poems speak for themselves:

The Breakfast Nook

the vision comes
twice
the object out of context:
first ducks
that look like snorkelers
black silhouettes
against a void
then at breakfast the next morning
the bowl that is no longer a bowl
but a white sound
swirling into

a depression
of unspeakable depth
the tea
a brown ocean
reflecting eight moons
my hand
a crippled starfish
naked, albino
floating up from the depths
holding a fork that has become
a long shining road
that branches at the end
into four paths
that lead nowhere

the spoon explodes
clicking and ringing:
bell sounds
rain on a tin roof
water beaded on flesh
and metal
domes of water
sliding down the side
of a glass
miniature worlds
distorted and luminous
all the senses systematically
deranged

the reflection is pitted
against the void
where no reflection
is possible

death can only be seen upside down
through a pin hole camera

the cat in the mirror
attacks itself

Mary Mackey
from *Breaking the Fever*

2

Fever

it lifts me from my bed
in an ascending spiral
whispering my name
over and over
like a disappointed lover …

Mary Mackey, "105 Degrees and Rising"
from *The Jaguars That Prowl Our Dreams*

There is something different about me, something profoundly physical yet not obvious. If you had just met me, you would never guess what it is. In fact, if you had known me for years, you might not guess. It's not a mental or physical disability or even what my health plan calls a "pre-existing condition," but from the time I was six months old, it has been powerful, recurrent, and one of the main things that has made me into a poet.

Put simply, in a way that doesn't begin to explain it: I run high fevers. Very high. Near-death-experience-high fevers. This does not happen all the time. In fact it happens rarely and has never been caused twice by the same illness. Yet, in the course of my life, on seven or eight occasions when I fell ill with a sore throat, flu, measles, food poisoning, pneumonia, or something else that ordinarily would only have only sent me to bed with a box of tissues, my body temperature has suddenly climbed to 107 degrees Fahrenheit, perhaps on one or two occasions even a bit higher.

107° F. (42° C). Let's pause and contemplate the implications of that number.

Brain damage and death occur if the body's temperature stays above 107.6° for an extended period of time—say twenty-four hours. At 106° you can experience fever-induced convulsions. This can even happen at 104°. In fact, if your temperature is only 103° (39.4° C) for three days or more, it's considered serious enough to warrant a visit to the doctor.

The first time I experienced one of these extremely high fevers, it almost killed me. It was 1945, World War II was still going on, and I was six months old; so I don't remember any of the details, but I was told I turned blue and went into convulsions. According to my mother, she and my father rushed me to Massachusetts General Hospital through a Boston blizzard, dodging snowplows and sliding around on black ice like people competing in a macabre bobsled race.

Despite the fact that they reached the hospital in one piece and in record time, I probably would have died except that my father, an Army doctor, had access to penicillin—a drug not at the time available to civilians. Antibiotic resistance was in its infancy, so the few antibiotics that existed promptly killed anything, which is why I lived long enough to become a poet instead of becoming an infant mortality statistic.

But fever was not done with me. The next time I nearly died from a high fever was just before my third birthday. I remember the experience well, because it was the first time I saw how thin and bright the world could be. I remember lying on a green couch in an over-heated room. It must have been winter, because frost coated the window-panes, and snow lay on the bare branches of the trees in big lumps. My mother had given me a bottle of Coca-Cola on the principle that I needed to take in more fluids. My temperature must have been somewhere between 105° and 106° Fahrenheit, because I was already experiencing that wonderful, detached floating feeling I always get above 105°.

Just for the record, the path from 98.6° to 105° is nasty: filled with aches, pains, uncontrolled shaking, and the pure misery of sickness; but once you reach 105° everything changes. You start to feel irrationally happy. Your body becomes light and buoyant. By the time you get to 106° you begin to discover that you are incapable of worrying, even though everyone around you is frantic with fear.

The best is yet to come. Teetering on the edge of 107° brings the real poetic gifts, because a fever that high does strange things to your brain.

As I lay on that green couch, a warm golden light—the kind you only see for a few moments at sunset—flooded the living room. My parents moved toward me so slowly that I could see their clothing billow out and collapse in an invisible wind. Bending over me, they lost their faces and floated toward the ceiling like huge birds. The Coke bottle on the coffee table multiplied into dozens of Coke bottles, which flew up and circled in a huge glassy aura over their heads.

Light weaved around the molding and splayed across the ceiling like spilled glue. Behind my parents' heads, the golden light turned into a veil composed of long, multi-colored ribbons that danced in an invisible wind. The veil expanded, consuming the green couch, the blankets, the windows, and my parents. Suddenly it parted, and I saw trees with red and gold leaves (impossible because it was the dead of winter), and little children holding out their hands and calling to me to come play with them.

I couldn't have had much of a vocabulary at that age. Nevertheless, words streamed into my mind and came out of my mouth, combining and re-combining into entirely new things. I believe this was the moment when I was given the gift of poetry—a gift which I did not yet have the skill or understanding to use, but a gift nevertheless.

My parents must have been terrified, but I wasn't. I don't remember much about what happened next except that I fought them when they tried to bring my fever down. I wanted to go on floating in the warm, golden light, and even though I wasn't old enough to read a thermometer, I somehow knew that on the downside of this fever lay sickness, misery, and a gray nausea that would smother my joy like an itchy wool blanket.

I've captured this best in a poem entitled *Breaking the Fever* in my collection by the same name. In it, you can see the childhood experience I just described transformed into poetry.

Breaking The Fever

When I was young
fevers were attacked
the grown-ups would rub you
with alcohol
wrap you in wet sheets
refuse you blankets
fan you, feed you aspirin
plunge your wrists in cold water

they knew fever had to be fought
because it let children see
forbidden things
At 105 I would start to hear voices
soft and lulling
at 106 the faces would appear
swimming around me

stretching out their hands
they would gesture to me
to join them

I was always very happy then
floating out on the warm brink
of the world

the fever children
would sing in high voices
liquid like silver bells
come with us
they would say
come play, Mary
and they would show me
maple trees turning red and gold
long aisles of sunlight
and woods that glowed and trembled

My body would start to come apart
very gently like milkweed fluff
and I would begin
to rise up toward their
hands
but always at the last moment
the dark circles
of the grown-ups' faces
would force me back down
and their fear would pin my chest
to the mattress
like black crystal paperweights

They would force more aspirin on me
more ice and alcohol rubs
more wet sheets
and if that didn't work
they would lift my naked body
and plunge it into a tub of cold water
ignoring my screams

Come back
they would plead
come back
come back
and my fever would buckle
and snap like the spine
of a beautiful snake
crushed under a boot

Then the fever children
would abandon me
and I would be left in a world
of ordinary things:
light bulbs
used Kleenex
hissing radiators
thermometers

I would see my mother's pale
terrified face
and my stuffed animals

and my brother's crib
and my precious fever would lie
broken in a thousand bits
with no way to put it back together
and I could never explain
how kind it had been
and how foolish we were to fear it

"Breaking the Fever" is a poem suffused with elation and regret, one in which I have used metaphors to suggest the way things felt rather than the way they literally were. At several points, it touches the wordless whole, then backs off into the specific. It also draws on other elements, both personal and general, which reinforce the central themes.

Take, for example, the reference in the fifth verse to "black crystal paperweights." My mother collected crystal paperweights and kept them on a table near her until the day she died. Each polished, glittering ball appeared to be a world in itself. When I stared at them, admiring the swirls of color and the glassy depths of transparency, I often had the feeling I was seeing slightly alternate realities, miniature universes salvaged from dreams. I knew for an absolute fact that this was not true, yet I remained fascinated with them.

At the same time, they had a dark side. Paperweights, by their very nature, hold floating things down; so if you are a child happily floating in golden light with a high fever, and your mother puts a crystal paperweight on your chest, you will fall back to earth where everything is ordinary and unenchanted.

Shall we talk crystal balls? Shall we talk covert references to divination (which I don't believe in)? Shall we explore why my mother was constantly talking about who she would leave those paperweights to when she died, and why she selected me?

There is hardly a line in "Breaking the Fever" that I could not write five paragraphs about in the course of attempting to unravel its psychological, social, and linguistic, double/triple/octuple meanings. To say that "this is a poem about not fearing death," is to reduce "Breaking the Fever" to a cartoon-like image of itself. It's more than that. It's a voyage to the edge and back. It's rational, and at the same time illogical. I select the words intentionally with extreme care and at the same time grab them randomly as they float up from the depths of my subconscious.

Poetry—at least my poetry—contains contradiction. Poetry thrives on ambiguity. Poetry continues after logic ends. I think of poetry as a place where you float down a river and fall off the map.

3

Falling

a cama vira/ the bed turns over

o quarto vira/

the room turns over

look how quickly

we can fall

into darkness

Mary Mackey, "Vertigo"
from *The Jaguars That Prowl Our Dreams*

At the peak of each fever—both as a child and later as an adult—I felt no fear, no anxiety, no dread. I knew I was probably dying, but I didn't care. As far as I was concerned, I was floating in a cocoon of warmth and light, and I wanted to stay there. My mind seemed super-charged with strength and vitality. Ideas and images floated up from my subconscious like bubbles coming to the surface from the depths of a vast sea of creative energy. I was too busy telling myself stories, speaking in verse, creating the plots for novels I would never write, screenplays I would never begin. When I paused to contemplate the possibility of my own death, I was not terrified. I was simply curious. What would happen if my fever continued to rise? What would I see at 108? What would I feel? I'd always liked foreign travel. When I died, would there be a vast new world out there waiting to be explored, or would there be nothing at all?

Fortunately, no one ever listened to my pleas to let my fevers go unchecked. My husband or parents, or, in one instance, my roommates would feed me aspirin and antibiotics; give me alcohol rubs; force liquified garlic, blue cohosh, echinacea, and Gatorade down my throat; and when all that failed, plunge me into a tub of ice water. In retrospect, I imagine some of my would-be saviors would have been happy to roll me in snow, but when you hit 107 degrees in California or a tropical jungle that's one remedy you're spared.

Blue cohosh is so bitter it makes quinine seem sweet, but nothing was worse than those ice baths. I hated them with a passion, and I'm ashamed to say that when I was a child, I often fought the very people who were doing their best to save my life. As I grew older, I became more resigned. I struggled less, but as they carried me toward the tub, or forced me to stagger toward it, all the peace of my fever would shatter, and I would be seized by dread.

Sometimes they would hold me over the tub and then gently lower me in. But whether they lowered me in, threw me in, or I climbed in on my own, the shock of the ice-cold water would make me moan and bite my lips. I would feel the edges of the ice cubes scrape against my skin; my teeth would begin to chatter; and my body would contract and shudder. Sometimes, when I was very sick and weak, I would even cry, not because of the cold, which seemed to be scalding me from neck to toe, but because I was grieving for myself and the happiness I had experienced only a few seconds earlier.

In those moments, cold and sick and lost, I never understood how lucky I was. The ice water always worked. A minute or so after I entered the tub, my fever would began to fall rapidly, and as it fell, I would fall with it, back into sickness, shaking, and misery; back into the ordinary world where objects didn't change shape, golden leaves didn't appear on the bare branches of winter trees, and words didn't spontaneously form rhymed couplets and stream out of my mouth. I would fall into a rational understanding of what it meant that I had nearly died, and suddenly I would be possessed by a fear of not existing, of being erased or forever floating in some dark, cold void, utterly alone.

Without this descent into darkness, my poems would have been like unsalted bread: pleasant but unsatisfying. Without a sense of my own mortality, without the clear, profound, inescapable, terrifying knowledge that everything could change in a heartbeat, or in the ceasing of my own heart, I would not have valued the ordinary world so much or been so attuned to the beauty of nature. The fear of death made life precious. It taught me empathy and compassion. It gave my poetry depth.

Of course fever is not the only source of the dark undercurrents in my work. From the time I was two years old until I turned forty, my life was often difficult to the point of seeming impossible. Bad things happened, and suffering sought me out, often taking me by surprise. Sometimes it came quickly and left in a few hours. Sometimes it dwelt with me for weeks. Once it claimed me for over a year and then gnawed at me for twenty more.

But with the pain came a great outpouring of poems. These poems were not necessarily autobiographical, nor were they always sad. Some were ecstatic, some angry, some triumphant, some created imaginary worlds, some were even joyful.

Try it this way: Think of a dozen boxes of jigsaw puzzles mixed together, a piece of sky here, a shard of a river, a fragment of a human face. Something dark, something light, something terrifying, something exhilarating, something that when turned into a poem suggests a greater whole without forcing you to see only the words on the page.

Who would Saint John of the Cross have been without his Dark Night of Soul? Who would Mirabai have been without her desperate longing for Krishna, her "Dark One?" Who would I have been if I had had an easy life? Not a poet, certainly.

All things considered, I believe I have been fortunate. I survived, healed, and received great gifts. The ecstatic, creative side of fever changed the way I saw the world and became one of the primary sources of inspiration for my poetry. Those dark moments, so necessary yet so unwanted, never overwhelmed me. Instead they were the greatest of teachers in a school no one goes to willingly.

Some of the light from those high fevers has stayed with me. If I look intently, I can still see the shining in ordinary things—trees and stones, and human faces, and the great arc of the sky that constantly hovers above me trembling with a clear radiance that is beautiful beyond description. Perhaps this is what artists see. Perhaps if I had mastered that craft, I would have tried to paint something simple like an apple to show you what I mean. But my colors are words and my brushes rhythms.

The darkness stays too. I could not avoid it, yet in the end, it also made me into a poet. I fell, yes. I fell over and over again, but in the end, I always fell into myself, fell into joy.

Raptor

> fever circles
> radiant and graceful as an eagle
> rising into the air
> with something clutched in its claws
>
> great journeys always begin this way
> first flat light   silence
> weight with no substance
> then suspicion
> certainty
> fear   flight

Mary Mackey
from *The Jaguars That Prowl Our Dreams*

4

The Geometry Lesson

Blown high on the wind unfurled
Gathered in masses of light
Softly through their numbered twirls
The autumn leaves in flight.

Reds and yellows, pastels soft
Shapes obtuse and congruent
Blown high on the wind aloft
Motions precise yet fluent.

Mary Mackey, age 11

I am sitting at a wooden desk with a glass inkwell sunk into its right-hand corner. The ink is dark blue and often spills into the desk and stains my books, not to mention my hands, my blouses, and even my lips and tongue when I lick the end of the steel-tipped pen. The ink has a pleasant taste, a little like metal and a little like blood. Make a sudden move, and you can tattoo yourself with it by accident.

On one side of the room are long, high windows, which stretch from floor to ceiling, topped with crooked brown blinds that come crashing down on anyone foolish enough to try to lower them. On the other side is a windowless cloakroom that runs from wall to wall like a railroad tunnel. I am at a desk close to the windows, roasting in the sunlight even though it's October, because somewhere beneath me a coal furnace is pushing super-heated air into a bank of hissing metal radiators that line the wall about three feet from my right elbow. It's very hot. Overwhelmingly hot. The skirt of my navy blue wool uniform is sticking to the semi-melted lacquer on the seat of my desk, and I know that when the bell rings and I get up to go to my next class, I will be leaving bits of blue wool behind like the tufts sheep leave when they brush up against a barbwire fence.

In front of me, a short, stocky woman with gray hair is presenting the basic principles of geometry. She has large breasts, which sway slowly like pendulums every time she reaches up to write something on the blackboard, and she is a kind person who is sympathetic when I tell her I have no head for math. I am good with words and famously the darling of all the English teachers, but I can easily add two and two and get five. In fact, in college I will do exactly that on a midterm exam and get C- until I manage to convince the professor (words again) that this was simply a mental typo, because, as he and I both know, no Harvard student could possibly make such a ridiculous error. But the truth was, I could and I did.

At the age of eleven, sitting in this over-heated school room, I already know I have to try harder than almost anyone in the class to keep up when it comes to calculations, although I can understand even the most complex theories if someone can describe them to me in words instead of equations. Often I don't see the numbers on the page. Part of my mind blanks out. Fives turn into twos. Threes run around like panicked ants. I multiply 142 by 3 and get 426, and when I double check the result, I discover that the number I was supposed to be multiplying was 124. Hand-held calculators won't be available for another decade. I only have my fingers to rely on, and often I don't have enough of them.

But to my surprise, I'm enjoying geometry. It's the first math course I've ever enjoyed, because it deals with solid, palpable things: shapes, forms, positions, angles. And it has the most wonderful vocabulary:

"acute angle," "arc," "bisect," "chord," "conic section." My favorite geometry word is "hypotenuse." It makes me smile every time I see it, because it's so much like "hippopotamus," the first multi-syllabic word I ever learned but so different in meaning. Not an herbivorous, semiaquatic mammal and ungulate native to sub-Saharan Africa, but the clean, straight side of a right triangle opposite the right angle.

New words always open up new worlds to me. Later, when I am grown up and have long abandoned my dream of herding cattle in Montana with a ten-gallon hat on my head, I study French, Spanish, Russian, and Portuguese, and with each new language I learn, I walk through a kind of linguistic door that opens on unexpected possibilities. A new grid falls across reality. A new word sits at each place the lines intersect, and all at once I see things I have never noticed before, things that have been there all the time that my mind has filtered out. Sometimes they are untranslatable concepts like "saudade" or "Души." But mostly, I see connections.

Yes, of course. This and that. Like. Similar. The same and not the same. They share some part of each other and yet remain wholly different.

Later I will realize that the common properties I see in disparate things are the basis of what is called "metaphor," but that is not a word I have stumbled across yet as I sit here in my starched white cotton blouse and blue wool uniform, breathing in air so dry it makes my lips and the tips of my fingers crack.

The geometry words for today, the ones the teacher has written on the blackboard are "obtuse" and "congruent." As in: "an obtuse angle is an angle between 90 and 180 degrees." As in: "shapes that coincide when superimposed are congruent."

At the moment she has a piece of chalk clutched between her thumb and the first two fingers of her right hand, which some stray part of my mind notes is exactly the way my mother has taught me to hold a fork. Her back is turned to the class, and she is drawing lines on the blackboard, explaining the Pythagorean theorem.

Although she has warned us that this will be on the exam she plans to give us tomorrow, I am not listening. I am looking out the window nearest me, the one smudged with fingerprints and dust. Outside, the wind has come up, and the trees are shedding their leaves as they always do in Indianapolis in October.

I've always loved fall. It's my favorite season, and this has been a glorious one. There was a hard frost a few days ago and the leaves have turned on all the trees. The maples are especially beautiful: red, bright gold, amber, some almost purple. They're magnificent standing there in long rows outside the school, their trunks dark and shadowed, their crowns like burning torches. The world outside my window is on fire with autumn, and the leaves are blowing like sparks, torn off the trees by a wind that lifts them up and thrusts them toward the earth in wave after wave so the air seems filled with falling embers.

Another stronger gust comes along, scooping up some of the leaves on the ground and tossing them back toward the tops of the trees. The leaves float, combine in patterns and recombine and suddenly I see ...

Obtuse angles! I lean over and take a closer look to make sure I am not imagining this, but yes. There they are like the lines on the blackboard only colored and in motion, fluttering and diving, joined to other irregular shapes in the leaves but still clearly discernable.

The sun comes out from behind the clouds, illuminating every-thing with that long, slightly morose light you only see on afternoons in late October. It's like an aerial road, a ladder, a glowing path. The leaves climb into the light. Drop away from it. Flutter back to the sidewalk.

I study one leaf closely, following its flight. I study another leaf immediately next to it. Maple leaves, both red with patches of gold. Pretty much the same color, shape, and size.

Congruent?

Perhaps. Almost. Not quite.

I feel a thrill of recognition, as if the inside of this room has joined the whirling world outside the window. As if both are for a single moment the same.

Blown high on the wind ... I think, watching some of the leaves tossed up to the height of the roof.

The leaves open and close like small flags. What do you say when a flag is opened?

Unfurled. That's what that action is called.

Blown high on the wind unfurled . .

I dip the tip of my pen into the inkwell, grab a sheet of lined paper, and write my first real poem. It isn't a great poem. It isn't even a poem that captures what I feel or what I'm trying to say about the identity of geometric forms and natural forms, or about abstraction and concrete detail. But I'm only eleven, and, I don't know such concepts exist. More to the point, I've never heard of fractals and neither has my geometry teacher, because the mathematician Benoit Mandebrot won't coin the term for another twenty years.

I only know that I have seen obtuse angles and congruency in the leaves outside my window, and that right now I want to write about those leaves more than I want to pass this class, get into college, or for that matter eat my lunch which is sitting in a metal box in the cloakroom and which (I believe) includes at least two pieces of my mother's famous chocolate fudge.

I want to sing the words in my head, words that will go outside and merge with the leaves, and then return to me so I can put them down on paper.

I return to my poem and make the lines rhyme because I have never read a poem that wasn't rhymed. I capitalize the first letters of the first word in every line, because I have been taught this is the way poems are supposed to look. One of Wordsworth's "Lucy poems" suddenly comes into my head and lingers for a moment like a chant.

Strange fits of passion I have known:
And I will dare to tell,
But in the Lover's ear alone,
What once to me befell.

Thank you, Mr. Wordsworth. But why did you capitalize "Lover?" I have so much to learn. So much craft to master. So many ideas about what poetry ought to be to get rid of. But I've made a start.

I have just become a poet, but I don't suspect this. I've never wanted to be a poet. I don't even know it's possible. I want to grow up to be a cowboy or an English teacher or maybe a veterinarian like my Uncle Mac out in California who dyes the movie stars' poodles to match their eyeshadow. I come from a long line of practical Midwesterners. I intend to be self-supporting, and I know you can't make a living writing poetry. But it's great fun. The only thing I've enjoyed more so far is climbing trees.

I put down my pen and blow on the paper to dry the ink. The radiators beside me are hissing like snakes. I've missed something important that the instructor told us. But I am happy. Utterly happy.

Years later, I will dream of the sugar maple I could see from my bedroom window when I was a child. The actual tree grew in front of a streetlight so it always seemed to shine even when it was winter and the branches were bare, but in my dream it is fall, and its leaves are golden.

As I watch, the tree in my dream begins to whirl like a single, giant leaf and then opens its branches in an embrace. *Climb me*, the tree says, and I begin to climb, finding a foothold here, a limb to grasp there, making my way slowly up its trunk, which seems to have no end.

Where am I going? I ask.

To your own death, the tree says. But don't worry. Every person born on this earth is given a tree that grows as they grow, and ages as they age. When you die, you find your tree waiting for you and you climb it into the light.

Will I end up in Heaven? I ask. Does it exist?

I am not allowed to say. But keep climbing.

The Outsider

where is that city with its bruised sky
endless soccer games
buildings dripping with rust and rot
air blued with the scent of bananas and mold
people who dance when there is no reason for joy

where are those long nights
dense, hot and humid
walls drenched in jasmine
silent parks where bands of monkeys
sleep in Jabutica trees
and malaria burns off the puddles like black fire

here in the cold lands the wind is blowing from the north
our gardens are dying   the earth is hardening
and naked twigs are whipping at our windows like headless snakes

Mary Mackey "Outside the Garden"
from *Travelers With No Ticket Home*

It's 1962. I'm seventeen, and I have just flown nearly a thousand miles
to begin my freshman year at Harvard. The college is in Cambridge,
Massachusetts, a town across the Charles River from Boston where I

know no one, have no friends, and have the social status of slime mold. I have not studied at an elite prep school. I am a scholarship student. No one in my family has ever had a building, library, lab, wrought iron gate, or even a bench in Harvard Yard named after them.

By the way I dress and speak, people can tell immediately that I am not from New York, Boston, Baltimore, Philadelphia, or Washington D.C. I am, in fact, a Midwesterner, born and brought up in Indianapolis, the very name of which makes my fellow students shudder and abruptly turn to speak to people who are obviously more intelligent, more worldly, and definitely more worth cultivating than I am.

To make matters worse, I have an Irish last name in a city that unwillingly received over two million immigrants from Ireland during the Great Famine and promptly celebrated their arrival by posting Help Wanted signs that read "No Irish Need Apply." My name hangs around my neck like a millstone. "Mary Lou Mackey": it couldn't be worse. The "Mary" encourages everyone to mistakenly assume I'm Catholic; and Catholics, I am surprised to discover, are held in contempt by my Protestant classmates, because to their ears that religion still screams "Irish shanty town trash" or, worse yet, "townie."

The "Lou" makes me an object of ridicule and in my junior year inspires three of my roommates to taunt me with fake southern accents. One is an aspiring beatnik photographer who comes from New York; one is a would-be anthropologist who speaks Nahuatl and has just returned from studying birth control among the indigenous people of northern Mexico; one comes from a family so rich and famous that even out in the Indiana sticks we have heard of it. When I come back to our room after class, they like to waylay me and chant; "Miss Mary Lou, come in out of the magnolias, honeychile, and bring us a pot of tea." They find this hilarious.

This isn't the only time I've been treated as an outsider, but it's the most intense, because for the first time in my life, no one seems to know who I am. My fellow students don't see the girl who at the age of twelve read the Bible and the Declaration of Independence and became convinced that all people really were created equal, and got into a huge fight with her mother when she called the local Methodist Church a "whitened sepulcher" on the grounds that there were no black people in the congregation; the girl who in high school was sent to the principal to be disciplined when she naively suggested to her American History teacher that we negotiate with the Russians to find a peaceful solution to the threat of nuclear war instead of issuing all the K-12 students in Indiana dog tags so our charred bodies could be identified when the Godless Communists attacked Indianapolis; the girl who grew up next door to two of the founders of the John Birch Society and rebelled by dating the son of the town socialist; the girl who wrote Bertrand Russell a letter thanking him for his support of nuclear disarmament.

All they see is a short, blond, white, female Midwesterner who must have been admitted to Harvard by some sort of clerical error since she so obviously does not belong within the hallowed precincts of an institution that has nourished Cotton Mather, T.S. Eliot, FDR, and John Fitzgerald Kennedy.

So I am an outsider from the time I arrive to the time I leave four years later. Yet, ironically, so are my three fake-southern-accent-adopting roommates, because all four of us are women. Harvard is not fond of its women students in the early 1960's, or at least the college appears to believe the education of its women is not as important as the education of its men who will (it is presumed) run this country as well as the rest of the world if they can manage to get their hands on it.

Women are segregated at Radcliffe, a supposedly separate institution, once called only "The Harvard Annex." Harvard, long ambivalent about the value of educating females, has imposed a strict limit of 750 Radcliffe undergraduates while admitting a total of approximately 7,000 males. On the upside, this makes it easy for me to get a date on Saturday nights, but the downside is steep.

There are Radcliffe dorms, a (small) Radcliffe Library, Radcliffe deans, and Radcliffe rules. Never mind that our parents pay the same tuition the men's parents pay; that we attend the same classes in the same lecture halls that the men attend; that we do the same work they do; take the same exams they take sitting side-by-side with them; and, like them, get a Harvard diploma: We are made acutely aware that we are not fully part of Harvard.

Our professors are not the problem. All our courses are taught by men, but as far as I can tell, they are fair-minded people who treat female students the same way they treat male students. I can't speak for the rest of my Radcliffe classmates, but in four years, I am never once sexually harassed by a member of the Harvard faculty.

I get William Alfred for Anglo-Saxon and delight in his imitation of Grendel. Giles Constable makes the Middle Ages come alive. Eric Erikson's lectures on psychological development are mesmerizing. My tutor, William Nestrick, who often takes the role of Winnie the Pooh in the Adam's House Christmas play, is kind and brilliant and has a major influence on my intellectual development, not only as a poet, but as a scholar.

It never occurs to me to think that I am being discriminated against because of my gender. I have been taught to believe that being considered inferior to men is the fate of women. Discrimination is pure, unmitigated evil. It's what is happening in the South where black people and Freedom Riders are being beaten, terrorized and murdered as they try to claim their rights as American citizens. It's what happens to an African graduate student from Kenya who casually takes my hand as we walk to the Brattle Theater to see a movie, and by doing so accidentally provokes a torrent of racial slurs and obscenities from passing taxi drivers and screaming racist lectures from strangers who confront both of us, threaten him, and tell me I am an indecent woman who should be ashamed to be seen in public with a black man.

Compared to what he and the other African students have to go through every time they step out the door, I feel lucky. Harvard and Cornell are the only Ivy League schools that have ever admitted women. Despite the restrictions I run into on a daily basis, I am getting a "man's education," the best education a woman can get in my era; but I am still an outsider, still a second-class citizen.

Female students don't live in any of the eleven Harvard Houses, which are the centers of Harvard intellectual life, but in dorms that are a twenty minute walk from campus, a trek which we must perform four times a day come rain, snow, or blizzard, since we are required to eat breakfast, lunch, and dinner in Radcliffe dining halls unless a male Harvard student invites us to dine with him at a Harvard House. No matter how cold it is, we must wear skirts at all times. (To be fair, the male students are required to wear coats and ties to enter their dining halls, but that's not an outfit that leaves you frozen from the waist down during a Cambridge winter.)

Women cannot even use Lamont, the Harvard Undergraduate Library, where all the books for our courses are on reserve. ("Don't worry," a Radcliffe dean tells me when I complain about this. "A girl as pretty as you will always be able to find a boyfriend to check out her books for her.") Since we are forbidden to step over the threshold of Lamont, and since security guards regularly turn every woman back—including on one occasion the future Supreme Court Justice Ruth Bader Ginsburg—no female undergraduate is ever able to enter the Woodberry Poetry Room where all the famous poets who come to Harvard are invited to read from their work. Nor do we get to read any of the rare, small press poetry collections or listen to any of the approximately 6,000 poetry recordings archived there.

As a result of being banned from Lamont, I miss Alan Ginsberg reading from "Howl." I miss Robert Frost. I am not only an outsider; I am literally outside when they read.

And that's not all I miss: The male students are often invited to dine with famous poets, but we women never are. Women, rumor has it, are not invited to Harvard dinners because "they bring down the tone of the conversation."

Sometimes the exclusion is more subtle. To get into the only creative writing class Harvard offers, you are required to submit a sample of your work. My sophomore year, I enter the competition with a seven page, surrealist, dream-like stream of consciousness piece that could be viewed either as a prose poem or an indication of an immediate need for psychotherapy. I am called in for an interview by Stephen Sandy, the poet who is teaching the course; and, determining that I am sane and not about to imitate Massachusetts' own Lizzie Borden, he admits me.

When I arrive for the first day of instruction, I am not particularly surprised to see that I am the only female undergraduate currently enrolled at Harvard who has won a place in the workshop. The miracle is that any woman has been admitted.

Mr. Sandy calls all nineteen men by their last names (Mr. Smith, Mr. Roberts, etc.). I am known as "Mary" (having dropped the "Lou" after the magnolia/tea debacle). But what I am called turns out to be unimportant. What matters is that, except for using my first name, Mr. Sandy treats me the same way he treats the men. A fine poet, gifted teacher, and superb editor, he shows us how modern poetry is written, revised, and polished, often pulling intriguing tricks like passing off a poem by Robert Frost as something one of us has written and asking us to evaluate it.

Thanks to being banned from the Woodberry Room combined with Harvard's penchant for only teaching poets who are either long dead or recently expired, I come into Mr. Sandy's class not knowing a great deal about modern poetry. I can recite the Prologue to *The Canterbury Tales* in Middle English and even make my way around an Anglo-Saxon version of *Beowulf* with a good dictionary in hand, but I have never read Robert Lowell's confessional poetry nor heard of Sylvia Plath or Elizabeth Bishop.

Mr. Sandy opens a door for me. He shows me what poetry is, here and now in 1963. I am weary of being an outsider. I want my poems to be accepted, praised, published. Realizing that if I start imitating famous modern poets, I may have a chance to shine, I take "The Emperor of Ice Cream" by Wallace Stevens and reverse engineer it. The result is a poem I entitle "The Death of Mabel Donahue," by using my maternal grandmother's first name and opening the Boston Telephone Directory at random to the D's.

The poem is a great success. Everyone in the class thinks it's brilliant, including Mr. Sandy, who gives me an A and suggests I submit it to Harvard's undergraduate literary magazine, *The Harvard Advocate*. I submit it. *The Advocate* accepts it, and in the spring of 1964, for the first time, something I have written is actually published. I am thrilled. Not only is one of my poems forever enshrined in a publication that has published T. S. Eliot, e.e. cummings, Robert Bly, Donald Hall, and other poets so renowned that it gives me shivers to contemplate them, the editors of *The Harvard Advocate* invite me to do my first poetry reading as part of the launch of the 1964 issue. But as it turns out, none of this is a good thing, because in order to get published and be accepted, I have given up my own voice and learned that I can only succeed by imitating famous men.

I am not a rebel by nature. If at that point, Harvard had offered me mentors and more formal instruction in the craft of writing, if I could have taken a workshop with a famous poet like Robert Lowell, or been permitted to work on *The Advocate* and, perhaps, by the time I was a senior, become its poetry editor, I would have leapt at these opportunities without a backward glance, and gone on imitating male poets, perhaps never fully realizing that I was not a man and never would be, and that there was only room in the world for one Wallace Stevens, one T.S. Eliot, one Robert Bly.

But luck was with me. I was a woman, and as much as I wanted to be an insider at Harvard and, by extension, an insider in the world of great poets, it was never going to happen. I had no mentors. No famous male poet offered to take me under his wing. In nearly a hundred years, no woman had ever edited *The Advocate*, and until recently, the magazine had published only a few poems by women, since women poets, commonly known as "poetesses," were thought to possess both inferior talents and inferior poetic skills, and were often mocked for supposedly writing verse on the level of that found in Hallmark Greeting cards.

The barriers, exclusions, and mockery made me sad and at times despairing, but, although I didn't realize it, being an outsider at Harvard was one of the best things that ever happened to me. Rejection forced me to write poetry that was original, different, even eccentric. It made me pay attention to what I had experienced when I ran high fevers and, later in life, what I witnessed when I lived in tropical jungles. In other words, since I had nothing to lose and no real hope of success, I could write whatever I wanted to write in whatever way I wanted to write it.

These days, with those Harvard years far behind me, I like to think of myself as a member of a long line of poets who by birth or circumstances were forced to look at life from a different viewpoint. François Villon was so poor the ink froze in his inkwell. Blake sat in trees talking to God. Mirabai's family tried to poison her. Rimbaud was a gay teenage runaway. Whitman was also gay, as was Elizabeth Bishop. Paul Laurence Dunbar, whose parents had been slaves, died of tuberculosis at the age of thirty-three. As a young girl growing up in Chicago, Gwendolyn Brooks faced threats, insults, and vicious racial discrimination. Maya Angelou was sexually abused at the age of eight.

Yet they wrote. They created. They persisted.

I was always an outsider at Harvard, and it has served me well. So I offer my thanks to everyone who ever rejected or snubbed me there, even the three of you who mocked me so mercilessly with your fake southern accents.

Without you, I would never have become a poet.

Fado Tropical

O mundo do rio   the world of the river
is not the world of the bridge   not the world
of memory   *não o mundo do passado*
not the world of the past   *não o mundo da*
saudade   not the world of longing

beneath the pollen that lacquers the surface   be-
neath the light
that combs the water   something indeterminate
lies in wait
e que é   what is it
that swims like a fish but is not a fish
that eats bone and flesh but has no teeth
cold-blooded, intelligent
suave somo una pantra   smooth as a panther

Leia a água
read the river
translate

Mary Mackey
from: *Sugar Zone*

6

Up On the Orinoco

Up on the Orinoco, Rio Negro, Solimões,
Tocantins, Xingu, Javary
they're drinking the *bebida preta*/black drink
snake vine ayahuasca/yage/   blood of the great anaconda
with the smoke of burning rainforests in their nostrils
and *o gosto de cinzas*/taste of ashes on their tongues ...

Mary Mackey, "The Jaguars That Prowl Our Dreams"
from: *Sugar Zone*

His three-piece tweed suits, wire-rimmed glasses, and Harvard ties make it easy to mistake him for a Boston Brahman, and he regularly votes for the Queen of England in U.S. Presidential elections, but on the wall of his lab hangs a black-and-white photo that shows him standing in the jungle somewhere along the upper Amazon dressed in a loin cloth. He stares straight at the camera with a calm, gentle, rather Victorian expression on his face as two men, wearing nothing but penis gourds, blow hallucinogenic snuff up his nose through slender bone tubes.

Before I first encounter him, he has discovered wild, disease-resistant rubber in the Colombian rainforest during World War II in an attempt to free the United States from dependence on Southeast Asian rubber; collected specimens of the plants used to make curare—the arrow poison now employed as a muscle relaxant during surgery; re-claimed lost knowledge about the hallucinogenic effects of Psilocybin mushrooms and the morning glory seeds Mexican shamans called *ololiuqui*, and testified in defense of the Native American Church's right to use peyote in its religious ceremonies.

But as he sits down at the table beside me in the Home Hall dining room, unfolds his napkin and drapes it across his lap, he is not yet as famous as he will soon become, because he is Richard Evans Schultes, "the father of modern ethnobotany," the Harvard professor who "discovered" ayahuasca, the hallucinogenic "black drink" that the shamans of the Upper Amazon use to send themselves on vision quests. Of course, he is not really the discoverer of ayahuasca, because—as he always tells his students—the indigenous people of the Amazon have known about it for millennia. He is simply the botanist who first analyzed the drink, figured out what plants it contained (i.e. *Banisteriopsis caapi*, Chacruna, and Challiponga among others), and brought that knowledge to the attention of the world beyond the Amazon.

I have no idea that this balding, mild-mannered man who will have such a lasting influence on my poetry is someone important, but at Harvard that's always a possibility. I learned this the hard way. For the better part of my freshman year, I hadn't realized that any of my professors—with the exception of being better informed—were different from the teachers I had had in high school. Even now, when I'm a second semester junior, I'm constantly bumping into famous people, and it often still comes as a surprise.

Sometimes I literally bump into them, as in the time I nearly ran over Erik Erikson with my bicycle; and sometimes I encounter them and react with embarrassing naivete. Sitting here in the Holmes Hall dining room next to Professor Schultes, I recall every cringing detail of that evening during Freshman Orientation Week when, at this very table, I was introduced to David Reisman, whose *The Lonely Crowd* is still considered one of the most influential books of the 20th Century. Professor Reisman was the first real writer I had ever met, so when he offered me his hand, I took it and said: "David Reisman! I thought you were dead!" A mistake prompted by my belief that, in order to be called a "writer," you had to be long-buried in some place where you could cause no mischief just like the famous men on postage stamps. Sometimes, I think I may have been right about that, but, needless to say, Professor Reisman was not amused.

So I contemplate Professor Schultes warily, wondering what he might be famous for and what terrible mistakes I will make if I try to speak to him. I am about to say something profound like: "Do you think it will snow again?," when he smiles, pushes up his glasses with his index finger, and asks me: "So what have you been doing lately?"

He speaks to me as if I am a colleague instead of a female undergraduate of no particular interest, and I am overwhelmed with gratitude. I'm a very social person, and I like to talk. All I need is a little encouragement and I'm off and running; so I begin telling him about the senior thesis I'm planning to write on serial publication in the novels of Charles Dickens.

At the mention of Dickens, his face lights up. "Dickens!" he says. "My favorite author! I used to go into the Amazon with only a can of peanuts—because the game is so lean you can never get enough fat—and two books: a copy of the *Iliad* in Greek and a copy of *David Copperfield*, although sometimes, when I planned to stay longer, it was *Bleak House*. Which of Dickens's books is the subject of your senior thesis, or are you doing all of them?"

"*The Pickwick Papers.*"

"Ah, that's a good one."

We spend the next ten or fifteen minutes discussing Mr. Pickwick and his adventures as Professor Schultes, who knows all of Dickens's books by heart, brings up one scene in *The Pickwick Papers* after another.

As we laugh and chat and pass one another the usual Radcliffe Sunday fare of roast beef and Yorkshire pudding, I explain that my aim is to use my senior thesis to figure out how Dickens kept his readers' attention from one installment to the next, because I'm hoping to write novels of my own someday. I have never before admitted to anyone that I want to be a novelist, but Professor Schultes is kind enough to appear to be impressed by the literary goals of a nineteen-year-old. In the end, it will be my poetry, not my novels, on which he will exert the greatest influence, but I don't know that yet, and neither does he.

As far as becoming a poet is concerned, I will only have two mentors during my four years at Harvard. One is my honors tutor William Nestrick, who gives me impossible assignments like reading, in French in the space of a single week, every poem ever written by the Surrealists, not to mention everything Keats has ever written. (*"And I do mean everything, Miss Mackey, including those works of Keats only accessible via the Houghton Library Rare Book Collection."*)

My second mentor will be Professor Schultes, who in these more formal times, I never consider calling by his first name. His comparatively modest descriptions of his plant-hunting expeditions in the Amazon will inspire in me a life-long love of the tropics and a strong desire to travel where he traveled and see what he has seen. Without actively meaning to, he will instill in me a sense of the cathedral-like beauty of the rainforest; and that great forest, which I often think of by its old name "jungle," will enter my dreams, saturate me with its mystery and nonhuman otherness, and become the source for some of my most powerful poems.

And it will not stop there. There will be more. Much more.

But we do not meet in the jungle. We meet in Victorian England.

"Do you know what tomorrow is?" he asks, cutting off a piece of roast beef and tucking in.

"February seventh?" I am mildly bewildered by his question, because if there were ever a grim, gray, miserable week in Cambridge without any holidays worth mentioning, it's the first week in February when the snow is still black with soot, and spring seems months away.

"Yes," he says with great enthusiasm. "February seventh! Dickens's one hundredth and fifty-second birthday!"

"Ah," I say, feeling that this is a fact I should have known, and wondering where all this is going.

"You must come with me tomorrow evening to the Old North Church. We're having a birthday party."

"A birthday party?"

"For Mr. Dickens. The Boston Dickens Fellowship, of which I am a member, hosts a birthday party for Mr. Charles John Huffam Dickens every February seventh. The Dickens Fellowship dates back to 1867 when Mr. Dickens himself began his Second American Tour right here in Boston with a ninety-minute reading from *A Christmas Carol* and *The Pickwick Papers*," He pauses dramatically. "Please be there at 6 pm sharp. There will be cake."

Stunned to have been invited to a party by a Harvard professor who obviously does not believe "women bring down the tone of the conversation," I accept his invitation, and thus, a little less than twenty-four hours later, I find myself sitting at a long oak dining table in Boston's famous Old North Church. Sexton Robert Newman, who hung those lanterns in the steeple for Paul Revere in April of 1775, is nowhere in sight, but present are some twenty gentlemen in coats and ties who have appeared to have adopted me as their mascot. I am the only woman at the table, and definitely the only person under forty, or perhaps under sixty. When you are nineteen, it's hard to tell the difference.

Professor Schultes and his friends have piled my plate with a large slice of white cake, which still contains bits of the inscription "HAPPY BIRTHDAY CHARLES DICKENS," and are now lustily singing "Happy Birthday" to an empty chair at the head of the table, where presumably the ghost of Charles Dickens sits, invisible.

Everyone is extremely cordial, although they do not offer to pour me a glass of the port they are passing around, because I am underage. Several after-dinner speeches are made in honor of the absent Mr. Dickens, and I even gain a minor touch of celebrity as the "undergraduate writing her honors thesis on our dear Mr. Pickwick."

It's wonderful, fascinating, and a little weird, and I love it.

A few days later, I am summoned to the office that handles part-time work on campus and told that Professor Schultes has put in a request to hire me as an assistant in the Economic Botany Collections of the Harvard Botanical Museum. This is not, I am warned, the kind of student assistantship granted to biology majors or graduate students. For all practical purposes, I will be a lowly part-time clerk and gofer. I will be set to work cataloging those parts of the Economic Botany Collection that have not yet been catalogued. The job pays $1.25 an hour. Do I want it?

I do indeed. I take the job, and for the rest of the semester, I spend a few hours a week in the Harvard Botanical Museum. To reach it, I take a shortcut through the Peabody Museum, a huge, red brick structure that contains, among other things, the last passenger pigeon ever sighted in the United States, shot, so the card beneath it reads, by a Harvard expedition—an interesting detail that many years later will make it into one of my poems.

My task during those months that I work in the Botanical Museum is to catalogue various foods and plants by writing their names on 3x5 cards which, in turn, will be placed in the multiple small wooden drawers of a large, wooden filing cabinet. The work is tedious but interesting. Harvard, which never moves in haste, has specimens left over from the Oakes Ames Expedition to Mexico, which as best I can recall, took place in the late 1880's. I find tortillas made out of ant eggs, rosaries strung with Job's Tears seeds (*Coix Lachryma-Jobi*), and a glass Ball jar that contains something preserved in whiskey so far gone it is beyond identification even by Professor Schultes.

One morning, I come across a large, heavy hunk of black sticky stuff that looks like a badly preserved fruitcake. Whatever it is, it has rested on a shelf in the museum gathering dust unnoticed since Grover Cleveland was President. When I turn it over, I discover a small paper label written in the feathery script of the last century, which says simply: "Raw Opium."

I have no idea how much a couple of pounds of raw opium is worth on the streets, but I rush the lump to Professor Schultes who immediately puts it into an iron safe where, for all I know, it still sits, available for resale should Harvard ever fall on hard times.

On another occasion, Professor Schultes gives me an entire footlocker of *Banisteriopsis caapi*—the main ingredient in ayahuasca—to catalogue. It's a woody vine, and it looks like an ordinary pile of dry sticks.

In my spare time, Professor Schultes allows me to audit his popular course on Economic Botany, along with my then-boyfriend who is a biology major, a real student assistant, actually enrolled in the course, and who, a bit later in his career, will be entrusted with dusting Harvard's famous Glass Flowers.

Professor Schultes's specialty is the human uses of plants (e.g. Ethnobotany), so as I listen to him lecture and take the labs along with the other students, I find myself chewing gold-leafed betel nut, eating popcorn, munching on dried plantain chips, and coming to an understanding of the history of dyes, resins, essential oils, and medicinal plants like aconite, golden seal, ginseng, licorice, valerian, quinine, and a whole range of others, many of which I have never heard of.

In late spring, when Professor Schultes begins to lecture on hallucinogens, I am initially no more interested in them than I am in turpentine, hemlock, or any of the other substances I never intend to ingest; but gradually my interest grows. I become acquainted with how humans have used Yopo (*Anadenanthera pergrina)* seeds, Ayahuasca (*Banisteriopsis caapi*), peyote (*Lophopohora williamsii*), and San

Pedro (*Trichocereus pachanoi*) to have visions and religious experiences. He tells us that Datura (*Datura metel*) is credited by some sources as being the source of the intoxicating smoke inhaled by the Delphic Oracles, that the shamans of Siberia ate Fly Agaric mushrooms (*Amanita muscaria*) and then drank their own urine out of special vessels to recycle the intoxication, and that Henbane (*Hyoscymaus niger*) was often included in medieval witches' brews and may be the source of visual hallucinations and the sensation of flight.

I never take any of these hallucinogens. I'm not interested in altering my mind. Fever has already done that for me all too often in the nineteen years I've been on this planet. I'm fond of my brain. I don't want to do anything that might harm it. I treasure sanity.

Besides, Professor Schultes repeatedly emphasizes the necessity of using hallucinogenic substances in a proper cultural context with proper cultural rules and protections; warning us that the correct preparing, mixing, and balancing of the plants that comprise a brew like ayahuasca is not a job for amateurs, since it is based on indigenous knowledge that has been passed down from shaman to shaman over millennia. The last thing you want is to be forced to call Boston Poison Control at 3:00 AM and try to explain that you need help, because you have just consumed a cup of tea brewed from an obscure tropical vine that only grows in the upper Amazon.

Plants, he reminds us, can be powerful drugs. Never underestimate something just because it grows out of the earth instead of coming to you in a bottle. Even taking a small bite of something innocent-looking like the leaf of an Elephant Ears plant can cause your throat to close up.

Yet, although I never sample any of the mind-altering plants we study except coffee, near the end of the semester I have a revelation that will affect my poetry as much, if not more, than my formal education. I re-read the accounts of the effects of hallucinogens, and in them I begin to find a kind of tentative camaraderie. The altered states described are similar, but not quite identical, to what I experience when I run extremely high fevers. For example, there seems to less joy and more terror in ayahuasca than in a fever, but the shamans of the Amazon, who believe they are transformed into jaguars who can prowl the dream world, report the same beauty and strangeness, the same feeling of categories dissolving, the same sense of leaving behind the ordinary, conventional world.

I think of the mystical poetry I've read and how familiar some of the poems of St. John of the Cross or Blake or Santa Teresa of Avila have seemed; how those poets famously struggled—and failed—to put their visionary experiences into words; how their poems have long made sense to me in ways that don't appear in any of the literary criticism I've been assigned in my classes.

One afternoon, I stumble on the fact that Santa Teresa, who was constantly ill, "levitated" during some of her religious visions and "spoke to God in the silence of her heart." I recall Professor Schultes' lectures on the auditory hallucinations induced by consuming plants like Zacatecichi (*Calea zacatechici*), the floating feeling I always experience when my fever peaks above 105, the golden texture of the light, the fever children who sang to me when I was three; and for the first time, I understand that I have been given a gift that, for better or for worse, will always make me an outsider. I will never be a saint—that's for certain—but likewise, I will never in a million years be invited to be Poetry Editor of *The Harvard Advocate*.

Chacruna Traz Luz/Chacruna Brings Light

I still have that photo of you standing on the bank
of the Juruá   naked   your hair tangled
your lips pursed in surprise   or perhaps terror

On either side of you   wearing only penis gourds
two Kashinahua (or maybe Tarauacá) are blowing
hallucinogenic snuff up your nostrils
either through hollow puma bones
or the leg bones of some small bird   now extinct
whose feathers you have woven into the wreath
you wear as a crown

on the back of the photo you wrote:
Chacruna traz luz/Chacruna brings light
Huaira, Punga Amarillo, Capirona, Lopuna Blanca,
Challucahaki, Camu camu

the head spirits are starting to speak
my body is dissolving

and then   in an almost indecipherable scrawl:
get me out of here!

Mary Mackey
from: *Travelers With No Ticket Home*

7

Unbecoming a Poet

Landing at the airport in San Salvador is like trying not to ice skate off the top of a frozen waterfall. The plane seems to hover for a moment, all four propellers turning wildly like synchronized eggbeaters. Then it descends with a sickening lurch, hits the tarmac, bounces, reverses its propellers, and taxis to a stop at the edge of a cliff. The view is spectacular. I can see tropical trees in bloom, distant volcanos, and, at the bottom of a cliff, the burnt-out hulk of a plane that didn't stop in time.

It's the summer of 1966, I've graduated from Harvard and been accepted into a doctoral program in Comparative Literature at the University of Michigan, and El Salvador is the first leg of my first journey to Costa Rica. What, you may well ask, does this have to do with my becoming a poet?

Nothing. It has nothing to do with it, because I've stopped writing poetry and, although I do not yet know it, I will not start writing it again for the better part of five years. The young woman who successfully imitated Wallace Stevens no longer exists. I've lost that voice and not found another. Worse yet, I have fallen out of touch with the sense of infinite wholeness that has always been my source of inspiration.

This resembles something akin to writers block, but it is not. It's something different. It is a dark night of the creative soul—only the creative soul, because during this period, I write scholarly articles easily, without hesitation.

By the time my plane touches down in El Salvador, I've already finished my senior thesis "Form and Structure in *Pickwick Papers,*" and seen it published in the scholarly journal *Dickens Studies*. In the coming year, I will write another scholarly article on "Rhetoric and Characterization in *Don Quixote*," and will be surprised when it is accepted by *Hispanic Review*, and even more surprised when the editor of the journal calls it "cutting edge." By 1970, I will have completed a complex, 350-page doctoral dissertation that takes as its subject the nineteenth-century novel and the Darwinian Revolution. I can write, yes, but in all those years, I cannot write a single poem.

I feel this lack of being able to write poetry as a disconnection, a dull ache, a background grief. To comfort myself, I write about how I can't write, stacking up folders crammed with pages of prose tinged with regret and despair until they fill three or four boxes.

The problem is that my rational mind seems to have taken over at the expense of instinct, intuition, and ambiguity. Without meaning to, I have lost—or perhaps abandoned—poetry and become a scholar who thinks logically, analyzes precisely, and reads more literary criticism and scientific journals than collections of poetry. I suspect this happens to many people as they make their way into the world of work and responsibilities, but I had never imagined it would happen to me.

The change in my creative life is accelerated by necessity—vital, immediate necessity. I miss the elation of crafting a poem, putting words together, creating something that combines logic, beauty, and emotional power; but I need a job. More than a job: I need a career.

Most of the women of my mother's generation married young and depended on their husbands for support. I have sworn always to pull my own weight and never be dependent on anyone. Although my father was the kindest and most generous of men, I realized at the age of fourteen that, when you have no income of your own, you are destined to be dependent on the generosity and whims of whoever controls the purse strings. My own family was intact, but I had seen too many women widowed or divorced, living in penury, trying to support their children by doing jobs that hardly paid them enough to support themselves, and I'd be damned if I'd join them in that misery.

Ironically, it was poets themselves who taught me that you couldn't get a job as a poet that would allow you to eat and pay the rent unless you were already famous. My sophomore year in high school, I went on one of my periodic reading jags with unexpected results. In previous years I had read all the *OZ* Books, the Bible, and everything I could get my hands on about classical culture including Ovid's *Art of Love* (the only even marginally dirty book in the North Central High School library) and Aristotle's *Nicomachean Ethics* (which I didn't understand). This time I plunged into the biographies of poets and novelists, determined to discover how their lives had inspired their work.

To my dismay, I discovered that, unless they had rich patrons or independent incomes, writers were often harried by poverty. Edgar Allen Poe died penniless. Dylan Thomas struggled all his life to make a living and wrote begging letters to more famous poets pleading for support. Balzac, author of over sixty novels and novellas, had a secret tunnel built into his house so he could escape his creditors. When his popularity declined, F. Scott Fitzgerald wrote and corrected Hollywood screenplays instead of writing more novels and died at the age of forty-four, a hopeless alcoholic. When Faulkner's publisher went bankrupt, Faulkner, who could no longer get a three-dollar check cashed in his hometown of Oxford, Mississippi, was also forced to turn to Hollywood to survive.

Being a woman just made it worse. Mirabai, the great Hindu mystical poet, was disowned by her wealthy family and spent most of her life as an itinerant beggar. Even in the second half of the twentieth century, a single, young woman living alone without an obvious means of support was surrounded by a whiff of scandal. Where, people wondered, was she getting her money? From her parents? From a secret sugar daddy?

Even in 1966, most professions were still effectively closed to women, and manual labor was reserved for men. A woman couldn't just set herself up in a garret, write poetry, and moonlight as a longshoreman, hod carrier, or grave-digger the way a man could. In an even earlier decade, when I was a girl, a woman couldn't buy a house or even get credit in her own name without a male family member co-signing the loan.

The message was clear: If you were a woman and wanted to be a writer, you had to be born rich, marry well, or live with your parents like Emily Dickenson and Jane Austen, and there was no way I was going to spend the rest of my life living with my parents. So at fourteen, I had made a plan.

I had looked at the sources of income open to me that would provide me with a reasonably comfortable life and time to write. The options for women were few: nurse, secretary, teacher. Of the three, teacher looked best and best fit my interests, because the long summer vacations would give me time to write.

Having dated a football player or two, I figured I was too short to maintain discipline in high school classes, so I decided to become a professor, preferably a professor of literature. Thus the good grades, the scholarships, the Harvard diploma, the fellowships, graduate school, and a PhD in Comparative Literature in the offing.

My plan has been working out nicely, so as I sit on this plane looking at the metal shack that serves as the San Salvador Airport Terminal, I have no idea that I am at the beginning of a five-year drought. I'm young, healthy, and the future looks bright and exciting. I can hardly wait to arrive in Costa Rica, see a real jungle, then return to the States, finish my graduate work, and become a professor.

I have no idea the price I will pay. I don't know that in becoming a scholar, I am unbecoming a poet. Unbecoming myself.

[This space reserved for a poem that was never written]

8

The Jungle

Crested Capuchin, Nectar Bat,
Three-toes Sloth, Golden Lion Tamarin,
Red-Handed Howling Monkey, Dark-Throated
Seedeater, Blue-Winged Macaw

great rivers veiled in steam
sixty billion trees
reaching toward a sky so green
it burns like copper

Mary Mackey, "The Invisible Forests of Amapá"
from: *Travelers With No Ticket Home*

Off and on, on for the better part of six years after I graduate from Harvard, I visit, and sometimes live, in the Costa Rican jungle, steeping myself in it until, even in the depths of winter, I can imagine the red glint of a heliconia blossom, feel the rough bark of a vine scuffing the palm of my hand, and smell the familiar scent of tropical growth and decay.

The jungle will test me, frighten me, console me, and change me. It will show me that there are actual places on earth as strange, luminous, and indescribable as the places I see when my fever rises above 106 degrees. In the jungle, I will fall in love with wildness, and this love for wild things will make me into a poet.

What was it like, this jungle that no longer exists; this jungle of the past that hovers on the outer edges of my memory? At present, it is no longer the wild place I remember, because in an heroic attempt to conserve it, Costa Rica has turned part of it into a national park where tourists can come to catch glimpses of animals that soon may join the great Anthropocene extinction.

But a park, no matter how necessary or well-meant, is a zoo. A wild jungle cannot exist where people call all the shots, and you can tour the trees and then go back to a lodge at night and sleep between clean white sheets. Broken off from the vast whole, a piece of that jungle I once loved now lies in benevolent captivity like a caged jaguar.

So what was it before, when it was whole? What was this great living thing that is now almost erased from human memory when it was untamed? An innocent green Paradise? A Fallen Eden? A steaming, disease-infested Hell that no woman in her right mind would thrust herself into, particularly if she were studying for a career as a professor of English literature and had no business being anywhere except in a library doing research for her doctoral dissertation?

When I close my eyes and look back over the years, this is what I remember: Not hell, not heaven, not paradise, not anything human or limited by human language. Instead a warm ocean of sunlight filtered through green leaves. A play of light and shadow. A vast forest that stretches in all directions filled with birdsong and the swift movements of a myriad of living things that fly, and climb, and slither. The tall trees with their pale trunks seem to breathe around me. The giant philodendrons splay out like hands. There is a low throbbing in the air that beats against my cheeks like a pulse.

This wild jungle is not simply a place like Boston or Bogota. It is a whole that transcends its parts, a living creature in its own right, a single entity so different, so far from cities and freeways, computers, political infighting, hospitals, antibiotics, and the threat of nuclear war that I almost need to invent a new language to describe it.

For decades I will struggle to find words to convey the sense of it to those who have never heard the rusty-gate cries of its parrots, walked through its lace-like leaf litter, or felt its gigantic trees towering over them. Even now, I don't know what to call it.

"Jungle" carries the sense of a hostile, mosquito-infested tangle of vegetation growing out of control. "Rainforest" conjures up images of a green park-like wilderness filled with toucans and hummingbirds and watered with soft rains that drip down through the leaves and coax orchids to blossom.

But orchids are parasites that grow on trees, and the choice between green hell and green paradise is no choice at all, because the untouched, uncut, untamed jungle is both beautiful and dangerous, ecstatic and life-threatening, dream-like and nightmarish all at the same time.

The jungle I see in the late 1960's and early 1970's is a "primary forest," filled with trees that have never been logged that grow by the millions in soil composed of the leaves and roots of their ancestors, spreading a canopy of leaves over the forest floor so thick sunlight barely penetrates in some places. Most of the life—birds, monkeys, insects—is up there in the canopy, so to walk through this forest is like walking on the bottom of an ocean.

Except at the edges and along streams, there are no impenetrable tangles of undergrowth. I rarely need to chop my way through with a machete. Instead, I can simply stroll along slowly so as not to be overcome with the heat and humidity while keeping a sharp eye out for snakes. I never need to run unless I am being chased by something, and fortunately this never happens, because if you are being chased by something in a jungle, chances are you won't be able to out-run it.

There is an almost dizzying profusion of plants and insects. Most of the animals have not yet been hunted to extinction or even greatly endangered. Sloths move slowly through the canopy trying to avoid attracting the attention of eagles. Florescent butterflies flutter in and out of the shadows. Graceful little agoutis peer out from the under-growth. Wild pigs snuffle in the leaf litter. Bands of howler monkeys swing from tree to tree carrying their young on their backs and letting out lion-like roars if you startle them.

Most of all, the jungle is a place of imitation, deception, and sur-prise. Almost nothing in this lush green world is as it seems. Pit vi-pers, camouflaged as leaves, slither across the trails and lie in ambush where I am least likely to see them. Green eyelash vipers pose as vines. Butterflies have large eye spots on their wings designed to fool predators into thinking they are owls. Sticks turn out to be insects in disguise. Lizards have webbed feet that allow them to appear to be walking on water. Termites hide in long tubes that run along the trunks of trees like miniature railroad tunnels. At dawn and dusk, the frogs sing so loudly we can't talk over their singing, which vibrates through the forest as if the tree trunks were being strummed like guitar strings.

In the jungle, removed from the support of civilization, out of touch with recorded history and the comforts of breakfast cereals, air conditioning, and instant communication, I come to realize that we humans—myself included—are not a special species. Perhaps, as Genesis says, we are made in the image of God, perhaps not. That can be debated. But in the jungle, we definitely do not have "*dominion over the fish of the sea, over the birds of the air, and over the cattle, over all the earth and over every creeping thing that creeps on the earth.*"

We're on our own: potential predators or potential lunches. And, as I quickly discover, the things that want to lunch on me are many. Fortunately, the wild cats—the jaguars, ocelots, pumas, jaguarundis, and margays—are either fairly rare or shy or else hunt at night when everyone except a few bat-seeking biologists is safely inside the field station behind screens with the door closed.

Those screens are vital, because of the estimated 500,000 species in Costa Rica, some 493,000 are invertebrates. Each morning, as I wake on my cot, gobble down a hasty breakfast of beans, rice, and coffee, and begin my tramp down the trails to perform various tasks, it often seems as if at least half those invertebrates are out to snack on me.

If I sheathe my machete and wave a butterfly net around my head, I can often catch a ball of mosquitoes the size of my fist, but killing a hundred mosquitoes does nothing to reduce the pestering swarms that follow me everywhere. In their wake come blackflies that chew off a small hunk of flesh every time they bite. And then there are the gnats, which crawl up my nose; the ants that sting like bees; and the vampire bats that can inject an anesthetic before they bite so you don't feel them sucking your blood.

The list of diseases I could get is impressive even in this era before Dengue and Zika have become common. Malaria and yellow fever top the list, which no doubt explains why nearly every older tropical biologist I met at Harvard, including Professor Schultes, suffered from periodic bouts of fever and chills. But with almost no effort at all, I could also acquire rabies, Chagas disease, leptospirosis, bot flies living in my arms and legs and cheeks, and parasitic flagellates if I were fool enough to swim in fresh water.

In other words, there is risk involved. Perhaps not much more risk than trying to ride a bicycle on a busy Boston street or take a stroll in a major US city at three o'clock in the morning, but risk nevertheless, and accepting risk, even on some occasions inviting it, is one of the things that turned me into a poet.

Usually, when people speak about risk with regard to poetry, they mean the risk of trying out new poetic forms or confessing secrets and deep, personal emotions. But the risk of living in the jungle is another kind of risk altogether.

If I hadn't been willing to take that risk, I would never have found one of the great themes of my poetry: the connection between the inexplicable mystery of the individual soul and the equally inexplicable mystery of the jungle, that is to say, the mystery of Nature itself, un-categorized and, like the visions of mystical poets down through the centuries, far beyond words.

Risk was something I was intimately familiar with. I had never been a particularly courageous person, but I had learned the hard way that my life was a gift. When I was six months old, I had nearly died. I had nearly died again at the age of three, and again on several other occasions. By the late sixties, I was fairly sure I would continue to run very high fevers, and I knew that someday, one of those fevers might peak well above 107.6 degrees. In other words, everything in my life from six months on had been gravy, but sooner or later the party would be over. So when I was offered a chance to live in a jungle field station and perhaps write about it, I compared the risk of dying or getting very ill to the risk of never doing something I had longed for ever since I sat foot in Professor Schultes lab, cast caution to the winds, and said to myself: *What the hell. Why not go for it?*

This is arguably the most important decision I ever made.

In Those Days Rivers Could Not Cool Me

I once lived in places
where volcanoes erupted   the water was poison
and the night swarmed with termites
that tasted like glue

there were rooms where I lay so wrapped
in fever that the fans overhead seemed ecstatic
in their whirling
rooms where I saw light the color of blood and bruised
plums   had hallucinations   dreams   terrors so great
they set me shrieking

once for 4 hours straight I spoke in rhymed couplets
and no one could make me shut up
until I threw off the sheets and ran into the tropical
night
like a woman on fire

in those days   rivers could not cool me
threats could not subdue me   I burned
and burned with illness   lust   and fear
and your lightest touch seemed like a blow

later   I cooked a monkey in cream sauce
and we ate it as jungle rats ran the rafters
over our heads the next afternoon I nearly
stepped on a nine foot fer-de-lance

only a mad woman could have loved such a life
but I did   I do   loved the strangeness of it
the non-humanness of it   the sure knowledge that
death
was so small and close it could buzz in my ear

Mary Mackey
From *Travelers With No Ticket Home*

Immersion

*Plants and animals pass into one another, a perpetual metem-
psychosis of protective coloration. Forms, colors, and patterns
converge generating an organic colloid; foreground and back-
ground blend by mutual accommodation.*

*A stick is floating down the river, drifting towards the pool be-
low the bridge. As it passes the edge of the gravel triangle (just
below the mouth of the creek), it suddenly turns, slides up the
bank, and coils itself around a warm rock. As it dries in the sun,
the bark begins to turn to scales.*

Mary Mackey, *Immersion*
Shameless Hussy Press, 1972

It's the fall of 1969, and I am sitting in the University of Chicago
Main Library at a small oak table by a large, dirty window that is
covered by a hefty iron screen. Unlike the window screens in private
homes, this one is installed on the inside as if it had been designed
to prevent people from escaping. The tabletop is scarred with the
marks of generations of library users who have marred its surface
with scratches, rings from illicit cups of coffee, and, in one notable
instance, small parallel gouges that appear to be the work of either a
frustrated, long-toothed graduate student or a rogue beaver.

To my left sits a large black plastic ashtray, because incredible as it
may seem, in 1969 smoking is still permitted in this building, which

holds well over ten million inflammable books and sixty-five thousand linear feet of irreplaceable archives and manuscripts. Directly in front of me sit a blank notebook and three refillable fountain pens. To my right is a bank of tall metal bookcases filled with books, which it appears no one ever reads.

During the three days I have been coming here to stare at the notebook and not so much as pick up one of the pens, I have not seen another human being wandering through this part of the stacks, and that's fine by me. In fact, I planned it this way. This is the Scandinavian Statistics Section, perhaps the most unused and least frequented part of the Library, a place where presumably people who can read Swedish only come if they want to find out how many bear fur cloaks, if any, were exported on a yearly basis from the eleventh-century proto-Swedish kingdom of *Sverige*.

The silence is so complete, I can hear the blood pumping through my ears. If there is a quieter place on earth, I have yet to find it.

I look again at the window screen, the tabletop, the ashtray, the pens, the battered books leaning against one another like drunks staggering home after a memorable Saturday night. I note all these details again and again, because I am procrastinating. I am about to do something momentous, and I don't have the slightest idea how to go about it: I'm about to write my first novel. And not just any novel.

It's a crazy idea, really: to write a novel that will create in the reader a sense of what it is like to be part of the jungle, to be as inseparable from it as the trees. Is it possible to use words to plunge people into a superorganism of almost over a billion parts that is a whole in itself and in many ways as beyond words as the landscape of dreams is beyond description? Is it possible to blend the vocabularies of science and literature, to use the vocabularies of biologists, zoologists, physicists, geneticists, novelists, and poets and merge them into a single, coherent whole, which, like the jungle is more than the sum of its parts? Is it possible to create a plot and characters that will encompass these ambitions—for all novels must have plots and characters?

I don't know, but I have just finished my doctoral dissertation, and I figure that if I can write a 350-page non-fiction scholarly thesis, I must have a novel in me, so I've decided to give it a try. The timing is right. The vice of focused rationality that has sustained me during my years in graduate school has begun to loosen its grip, and a host of ideas and images has flooded my mind. For the first time since I graduated from college, I have begun to remember my dreams.

I open the notebook and pick up one of the pens. I have no idea how or where to start, so I decide to begin with a description of the ashtray that sits at my left elbow. I will look at this ashtray intently. I will see it as if I had never seen it before, I will view it as an alien artifact created for some unknown purpose. I will describe it so that it cannot be confused with any other ashtray ever created. I will search out, find, and resurrect the way I saw the world as a very young child—a world in which categories did not yet exist, in which there was no context, no expectation, no reason not to look at the unimportant details of things as well as the important ones.

Beginning a novel about the jungle with a description of an ashtray may seem like an odd choice, but recently I have become increasingly aware of a strange phenomenon: If you look at any object long enough and intently enough, it becomes incomprehensible. Put another way, it no longer has a stable appearance, but will shift back and forth taking on different forms and changing size and shape as you stare at it.

I first came across this odd characteristic of the physical world as a sophomore at Harvard in an undergraduate Social Sciences course taught by Jerome Bruner, a psychologist renowned for his research relating to cognitive psychology and educational psychology. During the semester, Professor Bruner occasionally invited the class to participate in his research in harmless and fascinating ways that never caused anyone the slightest distress. This was in sharp contrast to the recent experiments with LSD that former Harvard Professor Timothy Leary had allowed his students to participate in—the ones that had gotten Leary fired from Harvard the spring of my freshman year.

On this particular morning, Professor Bruner had brought a series of slides to class which he projected onto a large screen. The slides were all of inanimate objects. When each slide first appeared, it was so out of focus that all we could see was a mass of undifferentiated colors. Professor Bruner explained that he would slowly bring each slide into focus and that we were to raise our hands when we could identify the object.

I only remember one slide. As it gradually came into focus, I initially saw the indistinct outline of a circle. With more clarity, I became convinced that I was looking at a beautiful aerial photograph of a great circular stadium constructed of warm brown tiles. It looked huge—perhaps it seated thousands.

Professor Bruner continued to make the image sharper. All around me hands were going up, but mine remained in my lap. A stadium. Yes, a stadium. But … I couldn't put my finger on the little thread of doubt that lingered in my mind. But … something.

At last the image lay before me in perfect clarity. I stared at the stadium, admired its grandeur, put up my hand, and Professor Bruner asked me what I saw.

"A stadium," I said. "A huge stadium seen from the air." There was laughter.

"It's a manhole cover," Professor Bruner said. The moment he uttered those words, the stadium shrunk, and I realized with a shock that what I had assumed was a huge object was in fact a fairly small one, and that for a good two minutes I had been staring at a perfectly clear photograph of an ordinary, slightly-rusted manhole cover without being able to identify it. The problem was: I had made up my mind early on that I was looking at a stadium, and once that happened, I had become trapped in the wrong category; whereas if

I had initially seen the manhole cover in focus, I never would have gotten the scale of it so wrong. All of which was exactly the point of Professor Bruner's experiment.

I turn my attention to the ashtray and stare at it just as I stared at that slide of the manhole cover: intensely, unwaveringly only this time instead of trying to identify it, I try not to identify it. Sure enough, within a few seconds the ashtray begins to shift and change and become both meaningless the way the word "the" becomes meaningless if you say it a hundred times and filled with possibilities the way all objects become filled with possibilities before you file them in the right pigeonhole.

A black hole. A void. A revolving wheel. A floating disc. An inkblot on the flat, two-dimensional surface of the tabletop without borders or depth…

I believe I am trying to begin writing a novel by freeing up my imagination from received categories, and indeed that is what I am doing. But I am also doing something else, something that will be so central to the way I write poems that it will change the whole way I go about creating them. I am teaching myself the art of entering a state of hyper-objectivity, a state of extreme focus. I am teaching myself to stare fixedly at the world and expect nothing but what comes from that staring. At the same time, I am re-living and re-learning the essence of metaphor that I experienced at the age of eleven when I sat at a wooden desk looking out a window at falling leaves and saw that they contained geometric patterns within their irregular shapes.

In the years since I wrote my first poem, I have become convinced that the element of comparison in metaphor is not an accident but is innate in all things. It is the quality of objects being able to look like other objects if you concentrate on them intently enough. So I sit staring at an ashtray, because I believe this kind of hyper-focus is one of the keys to the creation of rich, layered, complex poetry, and also, I hope, turn out to be the key to a rich, layered, complex novel.

Cool smooth blank a hole a dark spot shadow of a leaf trembling on one edge or do the edges go beyond out beyond like auras unidimensional so where it ends and the tabletop begins there is no way to tell and do you have to describe everything to describe one thing is there is no separation ... and ...

For the better part of twenty minutes I go on describing the ash-tray in the most minute detail possible, trying to see it without expectations of any kind, and then, all at once, the first lines of my novel appear beneath my hand like a shoal of whales breaching out of the ocean. I write:

Eduardo is drowning.
Rocking from side to side, he moves like a swimmer—head up, eyes open, fingers pressed tightly together. A neurotoxin is paralyzing his central nervous system, depressing respiration, sending his body into a series of involuntary convulsions.
(Closing my eyes, I stop the motion, reverse the sequence.)

I stop and re-read what I have written. What do I have here? A boy or perhaps a man christened with the Spanish version of my father's middle name. An *Eduardo,* dying of snakebite in a jungle pool for reasons unknown. A narrator of unrevealed gender who I suspect is female, one who moves between first and third person, between present time and memory, with no apparent appreciation that there is a difference between the two. A kind of baptism, a total bodily immersion that may bring some kind of revelation, although I can't imagine what that revelation will be.

Eduardo.   The jungle.   Immersion.

It's a beginning.

This is enough for one day. I close the notebook, pack up my pens, pick up my bookbag, and leave the Scandinavian Statistics Section to the great silence of its unread books.

I will come back repeatedly, day after day, to write more on *Immersion,* this novel which I will never outline but simply watch unfold out of my imagination like the blooming of a great tropical flower.

Slowly the plot will appear, at first in pieces, then as a whole. The narrator is a young woman named Kirsten. Isolated in a remote field station in a tropical rainforest, she wages a desperate struggle for intellectual, spiritual, personal, and sexual liberation from her lover who views her as a piece of property and the creatures of the rainforest as specimens to be killed and catalogued. The result of this tangle of jealousy, betrayal, and relentless tropical heat leads to murder but of an unexpected victim. And behind and within the plot and characters lies the jungle, that great living creature of a billion parts that Kirsten merges with, loses herself in. Becomes.

I write *Immersion* at a time when I have unbecome a poet, a time when I believe I can no longer write poetry. I write this novel while simultaneously trying unsuccessfully to recapture something important that I have lost. From 1969 to 1970, I put hundreds of would-be poetic lines down on paper, but they are lifeless, and none of them fall together to form so much as a haiku. I try to season my attempts with metaphors and unusual images, but the result is flat, contrived, labored, and mechanical. While *Immersion* flows smoothly, while I find writing it almost effortless, the poems I produce during this period are so bad they are embarrassing.

At one point, I even enter a contest I come across while, for some inexplicable reason, reading *Cat Magazine*. First prize for the best cat poem is twenty dollars. I can definitely use that twenty dollars, which is about what my groceries cost every month, but no matter how hard I try, I can no more write a poem about cats than I can write a poem about deep-well oil drilling. My ability to write poetry seems to have skipped town, and I have no reason to believe it will ever return.

By the summer of 1970, when I head to California to look for a teaching job, I have finished *Immersion*. It is not a long novel: only 126 pages, but in it I've done what I wanted to do. When I get to Berkeley, I make friends with Pat and Fred Cody, owners of Cody's Books, which at the time is one of America's great bookstores. I give them the manuscript of *Immersion*. They read it and are so impressed that, to my surprise and delight, Fred offers to become my agent—something I don't believe he has ever done before.

He is on a first name basis with most of the editors at the major publishing houses in New York, and he promptly submits *Immersion* to them with glowing letters of recommendation which say, among other things, that it is the most amazing, brilliantly written novel he has ever read. This is wonderfully encouraging, but it goes nowhere.

The editors send back rejection letters all of which more or less says the same thing: "Mary Mackey is an extraordinarily talented writer. This is indeed a brilliant novel. We have never seen anything like it. We want to publish it, but we can't see anyway to market it. It's too unusual. It's simultaneously cinematic, poetic, and hallucinatory. There's probably not a bookstore in the world that would know which shelf to put it on."

I read and re-read the letters of rejection and learn two things. First: if you want to get a novel published, you have to write one that will sell. Second: novels that sell are novels that are like other novels that have sold. Trying to re-invent the novel only leads to sitting around reading letters of rejection.

And I learn a third thing: In all those years when I thought I had unbecome a poet, in those years when I thought I couldn't write poetry, I had unconsciously been writing it, day after day, hour after hour.

Immersion, with all its passion, character revelation, struggle, quest for identity, and murder-mystery plot is definitely a novel.

But it is also a 126-page poem.

> *A mist net is strung along the opposite side of the river. Hundreds of fine black threads (invisible against the background vegetation) are suspended between the guaybo trees. Intersecting at right angles, two sets of parallel lines cross to form a huge rectangle, bloated into three dimensions at the center, stretched out along the edges.*

Suddenly a hummingbird appears, flying straight toward the upper right-hand corner of the net. As it strikes the webbing, it's flight continues for a moment without interruption. The bird moves forward rapidly as if unaware of the surrounding threads. Then, abruptly, the net closes in ...

Mary Mackey, *Immersion*
Shameless Hussy Press, 1972

10

Split Ends

hotel room interviews for non-existent jobs
and in each room a man sitting on the edge of the bed
saying   *you look too young to have a doctorate*
saying   *what about your husband? please explain*
do you intend to have children?   are you happily married?
what about your husband? would you leave him to find work?
really leave him?   what about your husband? and, by the way,
what did you say you could teach?

Mary Mackey, "MLA"
from *Split Ends*

A young woman clings to the face of a steep cliff, battered by a strong wind that is blowing her hair over her head and into her face as she clutches at the granite, trying, and failing, to find a handhold. The boulders around her look like boulders, but they also look like apparitions from a nightmare—skulls; demons; a long, thin body, hands clasped across its abdomen, face twisted in pain, head like that of a monstrous cat-like animal.

Just behind the woman are two safety ropes, but she does not seem to be tied into either of them. Her feet dangle helplessly over a dark void which may or may not be solid. Her face is hard to read. Is it registering uncertainty? resignation? confusion? She might even be experiencing fear, since you can tell that she has made the mistake of looking down.

She is frozen on the cliff face, unable either to climb up or descend. If she wants to save herself from plunging to a certain death, she only has one choice: she can go sideways. Directly in front of her is a fissure in rocks that forms a sunken path. The path leads to the entrance of a large, dark cave. She could edge forward bit by bit and enter the cave, but she can't even bear to look at it. She is convinced it has the shape of a mouth that will swallow her whole. She would rather fall.

This black and white lithograph of a rock-climbing woman was created by the artist Ruth Weisburg who generously allowed me to use it on the cover of my first collection of poetry *Split Ends*, published in 1974 by Ariel Press. But the poems in *Split Ends* were not written in 1974. They were written in 1971, the worst year of my life, when, like the rock-climber, I was at the end of my rope; and when—unlike the rock-climber—poems began to come to me out of nowhere with the force of a volcanic explosion.

Nineteen seventy-one was a year of cascading disasters. I was new to California, having only moved to Berkeley from Chicago the previous summer with the boyfriend who had dusted Harvard's glass flowers, whom I had married my senior year in college at the much-too-young age of twenty. I had written a novel that no one was willing to publish, but that was the least of my problems, which included grief, mourning, betrayals by close friends, an undiagnosed illness, the death of people close to me, impending divorce, and a sudden plunge into poverty that had left me sleeping on a mattress on the floor of a small apartment in South Berkeley, which I shared with two roommates. I had almost no friends, no prospects for getting a job, and I was rapidly running out of hope.

The war in Vietnam seemed to be destined to go on forever as men my own age and younger were sent off to fight and die in the rice paddies of Southeast Asia. The streets of Berkeley were filled with anti-war demonstrations, the sound of sirens, and clouds of tear gas that sometimes leaked into our apartment. A few blocks from where

I was living, police tack squads were regularly beating students to the ground, arresting them, and occasionally shooting them. The previous spring, while I had been sitting in the University of Chicago Library putting the finishing touches on *Immersion*, four college students had been massacred by the National Guard at Kent State. Eleven days later, at Jackson State, the police had opened fire on a group of about 100 black students standing in front of a dormitory, killing two of them.

I can read about these events now as past history, but to have lived through them is a different thing entirely. That year, the whole country seemed to coming apart, and I felt as if I were coming apart with it.

Little by little, I fell into a deep depression, a black, terrifying hole, which, like that cave that confronted the rock-climber, seemed to have no end. Times slowed down, and I slowed down with it. Sometimes when I got up in the morning, it took me ten minutes to summon enough energy to put on my socks.

Surreal things kept happening that made me feel as if I were living in a nightmare. One night, one of my roommates picked up a man on Telegraph Avenue who said he was a vampire. We all thought he was kidding, but when she started to have sex with him, he bit her on the neck, and my other roommate and I had to beat him over the head with pots and pans to make him let go.

I soldiered on, hiding my depression, looking for a job and not finding one. Because I had a Harvard education, a PhD from a prestigious university, and glowing letters of recommendation from the professors on my thesis committee, I had a number of interviews at local state colleges and universities, but the economy was not good, academic jobs had dried up, and the search committees, which were all male, were reluctant to hire women because the general belief was that any young, married woman they hired would soon get pregnant and leave to raise her children. Again and again, I was asked not about myself, my interests, or my qualifications, but about my fertility or lack of same, my plans for the future, and what I would do if my husband—who was an Assistant Professor at UC Berkeley—got a better offer, all of which was particularly painful since we were in the process of getting a divorce.

I flew back to Chicago to attend the annual convention of the Modern Language Association, which had long been a hiring hall for academic positions, and the same litany was repeated. *Number of children I might be planning to have? Fertile or sterile? Would I leave my husband to take up a position at university a continent away from UC Berkeley?* That last question was the trickiest, because when I responded, "Yes, I would leave my husband to take a position at another university," the hiring committees were invariably shocked by my lack of a "wifely" sense of duty. And, of course, saying "no" was not an option, because if I did, they definitely wouldn't hire me.

Having reached a dead end in Chicago, I flew back to California where I was interviewed by the chair of a hiring committee who immediately offered me a tenure-track Assistant Professorship. But there was a catch: I had to sleep with him. I told him he should be ashamed of himself, and said I'd rather eat dry bread in a garret than sell myself for a job. Instead of taking "No" for an answer, he decided I was a "nice" girl, immediately proposed marriage, and stalked me with flowers and incessant phone calls until I actually had to have my father back in Indiana call him up and tell him to leave me alone.

There's a happy ending to this story that includes me falling in love with a man to whom I have now been happily married for over thirty-five years; and ultimately being offered a tenure-track position at California State University, Sacramento, half-time in English and half-time in one of the first Women's Studies programs in the United States. CSUS was a perfect fit for me, a place where I was treated with respect by my male colleagues, never once sexually harassed, and where for several decades I had the pleasure of teaching Women's

Studies, Creative Writing, and Film to students from a wide range of ethnic backgrounds who were often the first members of their families to get a college education. But this happy ending has very little to do with how I became a poet or how that five-year drought when I couldn't write a poem finally ended.

Nineteen seventy-one was the year I didn't choose the subjects of my poems; the poems chose me, bursting into my mind like flocks of birds flying out of a metal box. In the midst of all my troubles, writing poetry was the only thing that anchored me to sanity and to myself. I wrote and wrote and wrote, and the words flowed so easily it seemed as if they were being dictated by a voice apart from me, a voice somewhere deep in my brain that finally knew what poetry was.

I wrote personal poems, explosive, raw, not simply confessional but tied to larger themes, wrote them in my own voice, the voice of a woman who was no longer imitating anyone. Poems with titles like: "Love Junky," "What Do You Say When A Man Tells You, You Have The Softest Skin," "Sexual War," and "The Other Side."

I wrote anti-war poems with titles like "Thank You, Tio Sam," and "This War Is Not Over," and recited them to thousands of people at peaceful demonstrations and benefits to rebuild hospitals in Vietnam.

I wrote poems about the plight of women: about sexual harassment and gender and racial discrimination: "Ophelia," "Psychiatric Emergency," "Why Women Need To Talk With Their Hands," and, of course, "MLA."

Stated like this, without using the words of the poems themselves, the titles sound as if some were political tracts that would have been better off written as essays; but that was not the case. Most of the poems that ultimately ended up in *Split Ends* were layered with double meanings and had surreal, lyrical, interior qualities, because what happened to me during that terrible year was an almost complete breakdown of the barrier between a direct view of that vast wordless reality I had experienced so intensely at the height of my fevers and the culturally-set categories that determine what we see, hear, taste, and feel. For the first time, I became free—as never before—to move seamlessly between the two.

A number of the poems from this era were good, but few of them were as good as the poems I would write in the years to come. I did not yet possess all the skills I would have later in life, and I still had many things to learn about craft and revision and about how to take a rough draft and transform it into a finished poem. But by the time 1972 rolled around, I had notebooks filled with hundreds of poems, some completed, some in draft, some merely a few lines scratched on a scrap of paper at 3:00 in the morning when the sun had not yet risen and I lay trapped in darkness staring at the ceiling wondering what the future would bring or if I would have any future at all.

So out of great pain came a great gift. Nineteen seventy-one smashed me; it tormented me; it brought me as low as I have ever been and at the same time unlocked poetic sources inside me that had never before been unlocked.

In 1971, I finally walked away from the safety ropes and entered the cave, I would have taken another path if I could have, but if I had, I might never have become a poet.

> … I took coltsfoot and barberry
> and conceived a fourth child
> she was born with a tiny ring
> of blood around her wrist
> and her eyes were as soft
> as new bark
> wildflowers grew in her footprints
> her bones were fine and hollow
> she flew over her sisters
> like a jackdaw

I called her Betony
and the neighbors said
I was mad

she will grow sweet to the taste
I told them
she will cure all wounds
she will be Betony
the spiked plant
the wood mint
the woman alone
who sanctifies

Mary Mackey, "Betony"
from *The Dear Dance of Eros*

11

Shameless Hussy

my feet grow hard as bloodstone
my petticoat falls off
I am naked and tattered
I chew a willow rod to a point
and spear my first trout
I twist my wedding ring into a hook
I survive ...

> Mary Mackey, "Wild Woman"
> from *One Night Stand*

"Tie your hair back!" she yells, tossing me a rubber band over the din of the press, "The last woman with long hair who helped me got jerked bald-headed by the rollers and lost part of her scalp."

It's 1972 and I'm in a garage in a small, ordinary house on an ordinary street in San Lorenzo, California, an unincorporated housing development near San Francisco constructed during World War II by a Navy contractor whose ideas for planned communities later produced New York's Levittown. The woman who just tossed me the rubber band is short and round-faced. She wears comfortable shoes and comfortable clothing and loves pastries, black coffee, and the paperback books that are scattered all over her living room.

When people first meet her, they sometimes mistake her for a divorced housewife on welfare struggling to support her daughter; but the truth is, she's in hiding with an unlisted phone number and an address she only shares with a few trusted friends.

Her name is Alta. Just plain "Alta," because she considers her last name, which she rarely reveals, a patriarchal legacy. Alta is the force behind Shameless Hussy Press, which she founded three years ago in Oakland, California shortly before being run out of town by an anonymous gang who threatened to burn her feminist press to the ground.

Shameless Hussy Press isn't just any press. In this era when no women serve in the U.S. Senate, Help Wanted ads are listed by gender, women often can't get a bank loan or a credit card without their husband's signature, and the literary scene is dominated by white, mostly middle-class men who acquire, edit, and publish each other's work, Shameless Hussy Press is unique, because Alta primarily publishes the writing of women.

Today, the first page of my novel *Immersion* is on the press's rollers, being printed by Alta when none of the big publishing houses back in New York would take it, and since Shameless Hussy Press is the first Second Wave feminist press in the United States and possibly in the world, *Immersion* is about to go down in history as the first feminist novel published by a Second Wave feminist press, although at the moment I don't know that any more than I know that *Immersion* is really a 126 page poem.

What I do know is that I have stepped into a community of women who for the first time are founding their own presses, publishing their own poetry, reading their poems to one another, and helping convince the male literary establishment that women's voices are important and deserve to be heard, that literary talent does not belong exclusively to one gender, and that a poet is no less a poet for being female.

Alta is an ardent feminist, and she has a genius for spotting great writing. She doesn't care about your sexual preferences, race, ethnicity, where you went to college, who you know, and where—if anywhere—you've been published before. Although she primarily publishes works written by women, she also occasionally publishes works by men.

From 1969 to 1989 her Shameless Hussy Press will publish one important feminist work after another: African-American playwright Ntozke Shange's *For Colored Girls Who Have Considered Suicide When the Rainbow is Enuf,* Lesbian poet Pat Parker's *Child of Myself,* Susan Griffin's *Dear Sky,* Mitsuye Yamada's *Camp Notes and Other Poems,* Paul Mariah's *Personae non gratae,* and, of course, *Immersion,* which is presently coming off her press page by page.

I am being published at last.

Recognized.

Welcomed into a community of women.

The list of women who help me and whom I help will be long, and it will span decades. But right now, at this moment, as a young, un-published writer, I'm at a turning point. I am not the kind of person who can write in isolation like Emily Dickinson or paint without selling paintings like Van Gough. I need encouragement and valida-tion to continue. I need some proof that I am not talking to the walls when I write. I need hope.

I catch the rubber band Alta has thrown to me and tie back my hair. I help her ink the rollers. The press clatters away doing things that I don't understand, but I continue to follow her instructions as the first page of *Immersion* is duplicated 1000 times.

There are two black and white drawings on that page. One is an abstract rendition of water; one a fairly realistic portrait of a drowning man. Both are the work of artist Madeleine Sklar who has illustrated the entire novel with a number of beautiful pen and ink drawings.

A few weeks later, Alta, Mady, and I will sit in a living room in north Berkeley fitting a green cover around each copy and stapling the book together. By the time the day is over, 1000 copies of *Immersion* will lie in boxes around us, and for the first time, I will see myself as a real writer. To my surprise, some people will actually buy my novel and read it, and in time, I will even find myself with a few fans.

As far as I know, *Immersion* will never make Alta a dime beyond her printing costs, but she doesn't care. She didn't found Shameless Hussy Press to make money. She founded it to let the voices of women be heard.

But this is not the end of the story, because the community of women that I have just entered will keep on supporting and encouraging me. Thanks to the publication of *Immersion*, I will begin to meet other writers including Susan Griffin, Marge Piercy, and the poet-photographer Lynda Koolish.

Two years later, in 1974, Koolish will help me lay out *Split Ends*, my first collection of poetry, culled from those dark nights when I lay awake in that small apartment in South Berkeley thinking that perhaps I had no future. The book will be published by Ariel Press, and I will begin to acquire a modest reputation as a poet worth listening to; and this, over the ensuing decades, will lead directly to my entire literary career—poetry, novels, screenplays, and all the rest.

In the years to come, I will move in a community of writers who do not ignore me, mock me, or insist that I imitate other people. I will read their poetry; they will read mine; and in the course of this rich exchange, I will learn a great deal, make lifelong friends, and finally stop feeling like an outsider. But that community comes in two parts: those who help me and those whom I help, and this is a lesson I will never forgot.

Long after I take that rubber band out of my hair and leave Alta's garage, I will create or join already-created writing groups, some of which I will participate in and some which will exist without me. In 1978, I will combine forces with Charlene Spretnak, Valerie Miner, Susan Griffin, and Jean Dickinson to found The Feminist Writers Guild, an organization dedicated to the establishment of grass-roots groups where women writers who have been isolated for decades can finally meet to read their works-in-progress to one another.

Sometimes, like The Feminist Writers Guild groups, the writing groups I help put together will be composed entirely of women, and sometimes men will be members. I have never believed that writing, not to mention life, is a zero sum game where, if women succeed, men must fail and vice versa.

In the years to come, I will remain more or less the same person who at the age of twelve read the Bible and the Declaration of Independence and decided that all people really were created equal, and that we can all accomplish more by cherishing our differences and working to help one another than by competing.

In 1974, two years after Shameless Hussy Press publishes *Immersion*, Maya Angelou will tell me "we all rise together."

And we do.

The Woman in the Moon

my great-grandmother
married at sixteen
a blue-eyed Irish woodworker
who promised to build her
a life out of apple wood
and cherry
instead he gave her
thirteen children
drank up the rent
and died of blood poisoning
while building a carriage
shaped like a shoe

for forty years
she lived alone
dressed in black
like a retired witch
in a house full of chests
and chairs and wooden clocks
waiting for him
to come home again

when she was eighty
and I was four
we met
her skin was so thin
by then that you could
see her veins like grain
she kept her teeth
in a glass of water
and her heart in a rosewood
box by the door

there is a woman in the moon
my great-grandmother told me
who carries a bundle of sticks
on her back

each month she swells
each month she declines
like many women
she has married a burden

and must bear it forever
across the sky

life bends us, she told me
my own life was scrap wood
my own life was sorrow
thick as a board

tell all your daughters
to build something better
burn kindling
not carry
keep one eye on the sky

Mary Mackey,
from: *Skin Deep*

12

Ghost Jaguars

This Is a Poem Creating Itself

Este é um poema criando-se
this is a poem creating itself *em um idioma*
in a language you don't understand

think of it as a dancer
whose face is hidden behind a beaded veil
uma bebida preta   a black drink that
lets you hear jaguars speak
a city seen from 20,000 feet
um barulho/ a noise that wakes you à meia-noite
tropeçando tropeçando   stumbling through the
darkness   knocking at your door

Mary Mackey
from *Sugar Zone*

Blue walls the color of a Caribbean sky; a ceiling blinding white as burning magnesium. Three windows draped in lace-bordered curtains. A bare, scuffed hardwood floor. The room is filled with summer light that seeps through the leaves of wild plum trees and falls like dust on a four-poster bed that's so short it looks as if it might have been built for a child. In one corner, there is a pier glass that reflects the bed. In another, a small writing desk with six cubby holes that look like yawing mouths. The desk crouches on its spindly legs as if it is trying to decide whether or not to make a run for it. It's the kind of desk Victorian ladies once sat down to when they wanted to write love letters, pay their bills, or compose obituaries.

I'm sitting at that desk in an old oak chair taking one of the last steps I need to become a poet: I'm trying to forge tools I will use for the rest of my life.

I'm still in Berkeley, but my roommates and their lovers are long gone. I'm living in my own house not far from the UC Berkeley campus, but far enough away not to smell the teargas when there are demonstrations. In fact, I only bought this house after making sure the prevailing winds would carry teargas in the other direction. I'm trying to live a peaceful life these days, and I've found that getting teargassed before I've had my first cup of coffee in the morning is not conducive to serenity.

In front of me is a large computation book. The book is open. The pages are blank. I write all the first drafts of my poems in books like this one. It takes me from a year to two years to fill one up. I know the pages of this book are marked with grids of light blue lines that form small squares. I say "I know," instead of "I see," because my eyes are shut.

I may look like I'm napping, but I'm not. On the contrary, I am actively engaged in one of the most important quests of my life—or at least of my literary life. I'm trying to figure out how to access the sources of my own creativity without destroying myself in the process.

In 1971, after five years of drought, I wrote over a hundred poems, but the price was high. Suffering, grief, loss, sadness, and despair shattered the barrier between my rational consciousness and the emotional, non-rational sources of my creativity, allowing rhythms, words, patterns, ideas, and dream-like images to float up from that great, wordless unity where they had lain hidden.

Now that I have put those troubles behind me, I want to go on writing poetry, but I don't want to go on suffering. I have come to believe there may be another path to the sources of my creativity, a gentle path that I may be able to follow without harming myself, one that might at times take me back to the world as it appeared when I was a very small child or perhaps lead me to some of the places I go when my fever spikes above 106 degrees.

Many things have encouraged me to believe that such a path exists; so for some time, I have been examining accounts of how people have contacted their sources of creativity, either voluntarily or involuntarily. I haven't been doing research for a scholarly article or marshalling an argument about how the mind works. I simply want to break down the barrier between my rational consciousness and the irrational sources of my creativity from time to time without ending up drunk, dead, depressed, addicted, or lying on a mattress on the floor wondering how long it's going to take me to sit up and pull on my socks.

The first writer I looked at was Marcel Proust, a man who seemed to contact his source of creativity primarily by accident. The taste of a madeleine dipped in lime blossom tea, an uneven paving stone—such trivial things became unexpected messengers from the past, bringing back memories in all their fullness, particularly Proust's childhood memories, which he suddenly recalled with an intensity that allowed him to describe them in minute detail.

I'm fascinated with Proust's involuntary memories, but they aren't something I'm going to be able to duplicate every time I want to write a poem. I might have to wait for years for a Proustian moment of unexpected connection, and that won't do. I want to be able to sit down in the morning, pick up my pen, access the sources of my creativity, and start writing. I don't expect to be able to come up with a poem. In fact, I'll probably be lucky to come up with anything coherent, but in any case, Proust's method is too random, too glacial. It's not what I'm looking for.

Still, Proust's epiphanies have started me thinking about memory and how it might be stored in the brain. When I was a sophomore in college, I wrote a term paper entitled "Cybernetic Models for Neurophysiology," using what information was available to me about computers and the brain. There had not been much, and the result was no more than a competent summary written by an eighteen-year-old who had never seen either a human brain or a computer, but in the course of doing the research for that paper, I developed an interest in how the brain functions—albeit an amateur interest, since I was an English major with no special training.

Over the years, I had continued to read about neurophysiology, primarily drawing on articles published in *Nature* and *Science*, but also elsewhere. At some point, I had come across an account of a brain-damaged patient who was able to recover lost memories in their entirety when researchers electronically stimulated his brain. Unfortunately I could no longer pinpoint the date this article was published nor recall its exact title, but the idea that my brain might be storing inaccessible memories had stayed with me. I had found it intriguing, particularly in light of Proust's description of his moments of accidental total recall, and I had filed it away for further consideration.

The second group of people I had considered were poets who used more aggressive methods to access their sources of creativity. In other words, poets who were not content to wait like Proust for accidental inspiration, but who were actively trying to contact the sources of their creativity at any cost.

What I found was not the gentle path I was looking for, but what I had come to call, for lack of any better name, "the path of intoxication." The number of poets who followed this path to the sources of their creativity was impressive. So many had lived miserable lives—drinking to excess; using drugs; voluntarily or involuntarily plunging into misery, despair, and depression, and ultimately committing suicide either by drinking themselves to death or actually taking their own lives—that one might say self-destruction is to poets what black lung is to coal miners: an occupational hazard.

Poe, Plath, Baudelaire, Hart Crane, Mayakovsky, Celan, Anne Sexton, Berryman, Yesenin, Mishima, Teasdale, Lindsay, Nerval—not to mention the Roman poet Lucan who destroyed himself in 65 AD at the age of twenty-five—the list went on and on. Of course there were a great many poets—particularly classical and academic poets—who had not killed themselves or even fallen into torment, but it was hard to think of another literary genre with so many victims.

Why had writing poetry taken such a toll? As I sit at my desk in front of this blank computation book, I suspect I may know at least part of the answer to that question. In college, in the course of studying French literature, I had come across Rimbaud's famous letter to Paul Demeny (15 May 1871). In it, Rimbaud explained what a person must do to become a poet. There is perhaps no better description of the path of intoxication:

"The first task of a man who wants to be a poet," Rimbaud argued, "... is to make his soul into a monster like those child-stealers who mutilate children to make them into beggars, court fools, and dwarfs ... The poet transforms himself into a visionary by a long, immense, and systematic derangement of all the senses. He seeks out all forms of love, suffering, and folly; exhausts within himself all poisons only preserving their essences."

For my purposes, the key words in Rimbaud's letter were "transforms himself into a visionary." Rimbaud and other poets who followed the path of intoxication were trying to become visionaries by breaking down the barriers between their rational minds and the irrational sources of their creativity. They wanted to write powerful, original, emotionally charged poetry, but the only way they had found to breach the barrier between rational consciousness and the irrational wordless whole was to "derange their senses," suffer, and at times even go mad.

94)

The path of intoxication was not going to work for me. I had briefly been there and been glad to escape, not to mention that I was apparently incapable of drinking myself to death or using drugs, since I couldn't even smoke a cigarette without becoming violently nauseated. Besides, I was convinced that leading a sane, relatively happy life was more important than becoming a poet. I had no desire to turn my soul into a monster, tear out my heart and slit my wrists to write poems. Nor did I want to write poems only because I felt like tearing out my heart and slitting my wrists.

I kept on looking. I reread all my favorite mystical poets including Mirabai, Blake, Rilke, and St. John of the Cross whose "Dark Night of the Soul" was the original reason I had learned Spanish. I examined religious rituals from a wide variety of different cultures. I read the poems of poets like Wordsworth who had been inspired by nature. I explored the basic principles of yoga and self-hypnosis, and looked into accounts of psychedelic experiences by people who had taken LSD, DMT, peyote, and other drugs. I even considered New Age practices like Silva Mind Control and Theta Cycles.

In some of these, I found small pieces of what I was looking for mixed with a lot of what seemed to me to be pure nonsense, but I attempted to withhold judgment. I was determined to discover how I could gently access the sources of my own creativity, so no matter how wacky a practice was, I was willing to sift through it looking for clues.

Gradually, I began to piece together something that I thought might work. The turning point came one morning, when, idly looking at the books in my bookcase, my eyes lighted on *Economic Botany* by Albert F. Hill. This was the text I had used when I was auditing Professor Schulte's class on the subject. As I stared at its battered brown cover, I had a truly Proustian moment. Suddenly, I recalled the ayahuasca rituals Professor Schultes had described, and the word "jaguars" burst into my mind accompanied by words that seemed to flow effortlessly out of an unknown source.

It's all there. No memory is ever lost. Everything that has ever happened to me from the moment I was born is stored away in my brain somewhere. I just need to find a way to get to it.

But what did jaguars have to do with this moment of revelation? Why was that word still repeating itself like an earworm? I was puzzled. The word "jaguars" seemed to be important, but it also seemed extraneous.

I sat back and thought it over. As best I could recall, Professor Schultes had told us that during ayahuasca vision quests, the shamans of the Upper Amazon sometimes saw themselves as jaguars prowling through another world of dreams and visions. Was this true? Was I remembering Professor Schultes's words correctly? It didn't matter. Even if my memory of his explanation was inaccurate, it was leading me where I needed to go.

Not real jaguars. I realized. *Imaginary jaguars. Ghost jaguars.*

Keys.

Jaguars are the keys that unlock the dream world for the shamans.

Maybe I don't need to break down the barrier between my rational, conscious mind and the irrational wordless whole. Maybe there's a gate I can unlock. Not a real gate of course, but some long abandoned place in my brain that will open and admit me if I find the right way to approach it.

Perhaps I need to create some kind of imaginary messenger who, like the ghost jaguars, will take me through that gate into the inaccessible, forgotten memories of my early childhood. A messenger who will, at the same time, protect me from the darkness and dangers that lurk in my subconscious. Or maybe it's not a messenger I need, but some sort of technique that will lead me into those parts of my brain that have been inaccessible since I learned to speak.

It took me months to put all this together, but at last, bit by bit, I succeeded. Now, as I sit at my desk with my eyes closed, holding my pen poised over the blank page, I am gently descending into the sources of my creativity using techniques I have borrowed, invented, or which have spontaneously created themselves. It is not possible to put these techniques into words, because they are leading me back to a place where words and categories do not exist, a place where they never have existed.

I am in what is called a "liminal state," straddling the threshold between the world of dreams and the world of waking consciousness. Part of my mind is aware that I am sitting at a desk in a room in Berkeley, California, and part is plunging ever deeper into a great ocean—boundless, infinite, and indescribable.

This morning I have a specific goal in mind: I want to write a poem. I cling to this goal with the rational part of my consciousness that holds a pen over a blank page. It would be so easy to lose it. To have my mind go entirely blank and silent.

I am not dreaming, and I am definitely not meditating, for although I have recently begun to meditate twice a day, meditation is something else entirely.

Time passes. A few minutes? An hour? I have no way of telling. Time has a different shape here.

After a while, ideas and images come bubbling up from the depths. A poem begins to form in my mind, not a complete poem, not a polished poem, but the seed of something. The poem does not come in words. It comes as something else: partly memory, partly taste and scent, partly as a kind of brightly-colored movie that changes and morphs into solid objects that in turn morph into abstractions.

Slowly the seed of this proto-poem sprouts and begins to blossom. I can feel words flowing through it, whispers too indistinct to make out, as if a great crowd has gathered to admire it.

Is this a good poem? A bad one? It doesn't matter. The concept of value has no meaning at this stage. Later, if what I come up with seems useable, I will need to craft it, polish it, work with it, decide to keep it or discard it. But at present, it only exists the way a wind or a breath exists—perceptible but not entirely solid, wrapped in possibilities, rising from the depths with bits of other possible poems clinging to it and rising with it.

I need to perform surgery on this gift from my subconscious: select it, separate it, cut it off from the wordless unity, turn the result over in my mind, examine it, memorize it, categorize it.

I cut here.

I cut there.

I include.

I exclude.

It takes on edges and endings. Solidity. Stability. Falls apart for a moment, then reconstitutes itself as something specific.

I remind myself to remember. Remember. Remember. I do not want this fragile proto-poem to be like dreams, which I forget as soon as I wake. I want it to be stored in my memory long enough for me to get it down on paper.

For a moment or two, I hold the image before my mind's eye like a minor moon seen from a great distance, bright and clear, shorn of the detritus of other possible poems, yet complete in itself with its scents, rhythms, and whispered words intact.

At last, I take a deep breath, open my eyes a little, and lower my pen to the blank page crisscrossed with faint blue lines. The image turns in my head. Shines now in its own light. Words crystalize around it and flow toward my fingers. I begin to write.

Ghost Jaguars

by day   you told   us   the dead crouch in the jungle
arms wrapped around their knees
heads down   blind
living in a great blueness
that expands to the horizon
like an infinite ocean

at night they rise
and hunt the ghost jaguars
drink the black drink
embrace the trees

we threw your *yopo* seeds on the ground
and trampled them
begged you to come back to us
but you had already eaten your gods
gone hunting with the dead
seen the sun rise and gone blind

Mary Mackey
from *The Jaguars That Prowl Our Dreams*

13

The Mystery of Creativity

Troops of Brightly Colored Monkeys

troops of brightly colored monkeys
hang from the branches of the Chicona trees
under the Barrigona palms
orange fishing spiders
with venom more toxic than cobras
are weaving gigantic snares
that billow like silver sails

why these strange creatures?
why this fevered nightmare?
the jungle says   *eu sou grande*/I am vast
você é pouco/ you are nothing
no one is going to save you
no one is going to helicopter you out of here

Mary Mackey
from *The Jaguars That Prowl Our Dreams*

A stretch of water lies before me, black and smooth as a mirror of polished ebony. There is no depth to this water; no ripples mar its surface; no school of piranhas rises to feed on living things that tread too close to the border between liquid and solid. Today and all days here far up the Amazon, a thousand miles or more from any city, I see only reflections that reflect themselves and then reflect themselves reflecting. Sky, drowned trees, clouds, air, water, vines, a shatteringly hot sun: I cannot tell which of these things is real and which is the mirror image. I am lost without a horizon, passing through a world of hallucinations that multiplies itself dream-like on water and keeps on multiplying.

The blue, cloud-strewn sky over my head looks exactly like the blue, cloud-strewn sky beneath my dugout canoe. The edge of the jungle where the open water ends and the trees begin rises above me and below me in two symmetrical waves of bleach-white trunks, curling vines, snarled underbrush, and scarlet flowers. I have never felt closer to the sensation of flying, not even when, in an attempt to learn how to hang glide, I jumped off a cliff in San Francisco with nylon wings strapped to my back. Nor have I ever felt closer to the sensation of living in a dream without dreaming.

I am exhilarated, almost ecstatic. After an absence of many decades, I have finally returned to the jungle—not to that Costa Rican jungle where I lived in a biological field station off and on for six years, for it has become a national park; but to Amazonia, the great mother of all jungles that stretches for over two-and-a-half-million square miles and includes territory belonging to nine nations.

This afternoon, I am floating on the Rio Negro, the famous "Black River" of Brazil that merges with its sister the Solimões downstream to form the Amazon River. Twenty percent of the water reaching the oceans of the world flows down the Amazon, and I am riding that flow—or rather I was riding it until a little while ago. Now I have shipped my paddle and stopped to float silently over the mirrored sky.

I stare at a wall of trees that lies some two hundred yards ahead of me. The trees look nothing like the towering giants I remember from my years in Costa Rica. How tall are they? Thirty feet tall? Maybe forty at most? Some are so short that they are dipping the tips of their branches into the river as if they were nothing more than bushes. But that's an illusion.

The trees are huge. Most are a hundred feet tall, some as much as two hundred feet, and they exist—millions of them exist—in almost complete solitude. No one harvests their fruits, or strips off their bark, or burns them or clear cuts them for a very simple reason: Every wet season, the Rio Negro floods an area the size of California for months at a time, rising sixty feet or more and sending every living thing that can't breathe water scrambling up into the canopy. There are no people living in the drowned jungle, which lies ahead of me, none for hundreds of miles in any direction, because right now there is no piece of earth high enough above the surface of the river that is large enough for a human being to stand on, much less build a city or a sawmill.

When I finally paddle into this drowned jungle, I will be floating through the tops of the trees, drifting from one to the next like a gliding bird, and if my past experiences are any guide, I will see more animal life in a few hours than I saw in months in the jungles of Costa Rica. But I am in no hurry. I am on an important journey, and I want to savor every moment of it.

This journey began ten years ago when I finally discovered the great theme of my poetry, the subject that formed my life into a spiral, drew me back to the earliest days of my childhood, and yet contained all the years in between.

In the fall of 1969 I had written *Immersion*, my first novel. It had been set in a jungle. Twenty-six years later, in the fall of 1995, after writing seven more novels and five collections of poetry, I pulled *Immersion* out of my bookcase one rainy afternoon and re-read it, and for the first time I realized that it was not really a novel but a 126-page poem.

But that was not the most important revelation I had that afternoon. As I finished *Immersion*, carefully closed its fragile green covers, and looked up, I found myself staring out the window at a cold, gray landscape. Dark clouds. Brown grass. Bare trees. A stiff wind that had set the dead leaves flying. Naked twigs beating against the windowpane.

I want to see the sun, I thought. *I want to feel its warmth on my face, smell the scent of growing things, breathe moist air instead of air heated by a gas furnace that's so dry that it chaps my lips and parches the inside of my nose.*

I looked down at the cover of *Immersion,* the one Madeline Sklar had created back in 1972. A naked woman—who looked nothing at all like me—stood in the jungle with an expression of serenity on her face, surrounded by trees, tinamous, eyelash vipers, frogs, monkeys, toucans, sloths, butterflies, lianas, giant philodendrons, leafcutter ants, praying mantises, humming birds, walking sticks, toads, lizards, trumpet flowers, coatis, iguanas, ferns, caterpillars, pit vipers, orchids, spiders, beetles, and even the odd mosquito or two.

I looked at the richness of it all. The living force of it. The beauty that came across even in a simple pen and ink drawing, and suddenly I realized that I wanted to be there, standing where that woman was standing. I wanted to return to the jungle with every fiber of my being, wanted to go back to it as passionately as I might have wanted to return to a lover I had left long ago and deeply regretted leaving.

Suddenly I realized I was in love. Fiercely, passionately in love, not with a person but with a living entity that was millions of times greater than I was. Call it *selva, rainforest,* or *the wilds.* Call it *ka'aguy* as it is called in Guarani. Call it by its ancient Sanskrit name *jangala,* or *jungle,* or just call it *a tropical forest.* Whatever I or anyone else chose to call it didn't matter, because it knew no human names. It was a living, breathing organism complete in itself: beautiful, dangerous, vulnerable. Capable of being embraced but not fully understood; strong yet fragile; understandable in some parts, yet forever mysterious in others. Capable of dying; capable of being destroyed; capable of disappearing from the earth forever.

As I put that copy of *Immersion* back in the bookcase beside my desk, I finally realized that the jungle had always been my great theme, the thing that took me closest to that wordless whole I had perceived as a child during high fevers, but it had taken me until I was fifty to write more than a scattering of poems about it. Why? Why had it taken so long for me to become the poet I was probably inclined to be from the time I was a child?

The truth is that even now I don't know.

All I can say is that creativity is a gift. You can't board it like a bus and expect it to take you wherever you want to go. It's ephemeral, phantom-like, ungraspable, and indescribable by its very nature, because it comes from a place where words have no dominion. Inspiration comes in its own time, often as a surprise and frequently in a language composed of images and faint suggestions that needs to be decoded. Creativity has an illogical logic all its own.

So, not yet understanding myself, I had become a poet, unbecame a poet, and become a poet over and over again from decade to decade. Finally after twenty-six years of not realizing that the jungle with all its great beauty and great dangers was the place where I felt the most complete and closest to the sources of my own creativity, I realized I had to return.

Yet returning was not easy. Even though my husband and I had been traveling to Brazil almost every year from 1991 on, it took me a long time to figure out how to get into the real jungle—not the jungle of tourist lodges and cruises down the Amazon on air-conditioned ships that sport their own casinos, but that remote jungle that doesn't care a whit about whether you live or die, that lush, green world where you are just one animal among many, adrift in a land beyond human words and human categories.

Now as I float on the Rio Negro about a thousand miles upriver from the Brazilian city of Manaus and about two hundred yards from the green rim of the jungle, I am finally going home.

As I dip my paddle into the black mirror beneath my dugout, a new poem begins to bubble up from somewhere deep inside me. Suddenly a light breeze blows across the water bringing with it the scent of leaves and mud. All at once the mirror beneath my canoe shatters taking the sky with it.

A Reunião/The Conference

When I entered the hall
they filled my head with birds
macaws   parrots   chachalacas

I could feel them whistling crackling
bumping into one another behind
my sinuses   the birds sang of love & death
poetry put in cages   people
who only wrote to mimic the sounds
of their own voices   rich women
who tried to buy prizes

but I wanted to hear the sounds of the
jungle   the vast humming of sap
running through ten million trees
the slither of the *cascabel muda*
the hush of a lone dugout canoe
riding the current   the silent running
of piranhas & pink dolphins
the ancient music of hot nights
drenched and burned
in the trilling of transparent frogs

Mary Mackey
from *Sugar Zone*

About the Author

MARY MACKEY received a BA in English Literature from Harvard and a PhD in Comparative Literature from the University of Michigan. She is the author of eight collections of poetry including *Sugar Zone* (Marsh Hawk Press, 2011), winner of the 2012 PEN Oakland Josephine Miles Award for Excellence in Literature and Finalist for the Northern California Book Awards; and *The Jaguars That Prowl Our Dreams* (Marsh Hawk Press, 2018),which won both the 2019 Eric Hoffer Small Press Award for the best book published by a small press and a 2018 Women's Spirituality Book Award from the Philosophy, Religion, and Women's Spirituality Department of the California Institute for Integral Studies. Her poems have appeared in numerous magazines, journals, and anthologies; been featured on *The Writers Almanac*; and been praised by Wendell Berry, Eugene Redmond, Jane Hirshfield, D. Nurkse, Maxine Hong Kingston, Al Young, Rafael Jesús González, and Marge Piercy for their beauty, precision, originality, and extraordinary range.

She is also the author of fourteen novels, one of which made *The New York Times* Best Seller list. As far as anyone has been able to determine, her first novel, *Immersion* (Shameless Hussy Press, 1972), was the first novel in the world published by a Second Wave Feminist press.

Mackey's works have been translated into twelve languages including Japanese, Hebrew, Russian, Greek, and Finnish. She is past president of the West Coast branch of PEN, a Fellow of the Virginia Center for the Creative Arts, a member of the National Book Critics Circle, and Professor Emeritus of English at California State University, Sacramento where she was one of the founders of the Women's Studies Program and the graduate and undergraduate Creative Writing programs. For over thirty years she has been traveling to Brazil with her husband, Angus Wright, who writes about land reform and environmental issues.

To contact her, sample more of her work, read her blog interview series *People Who Make Books Happen,* and receive her quarterly newsletter, you are invited to visit her website at www.marymackey.com. You can also follow her on Twitter at @MMackeyAuthor and find her on Facebook at www.facebook.com/marymackeywriter. Her books are available in hard copy as well as in e-book and Audible editions.

Mary Mackey's literary papers are archived in the Sophia Smith Special Collections Library, Smith College, Northampton, MA. Her collection of rare editions of small press poetry books is archived in the Smith College Mortimer Rare Book Collection.

Acknowledgments

Creation takes place in a community. I could not have become a poet without the teachers, librarians, friends, colleagues, and strangers who educated me, encouraged me, wrote the books I read, grew the food I ate, laid the sidewalks I walked on, took care of me when I was ill, comforted me when I was sad, and laughed with me through good times and bad. Thank you for helping me in more ways that I can name.

I would also like to thank Pamela Berkman and Dorothy Hearst who read every draft of *Creativity* and gave me invaluable feedback; Sandy McIntosh who asked me to write a short book about becoming a poet for the Marsh Hawk Press Chapter One Series; The Virginia Center for the Creative Arts; and my husband, Angus Wright, who—besides being almost preternaturally tolerant of a wife who shuts herself away for hours at a time to write—is always ready to read and comment on my work when I come bursting out of my study waving a sheet of paper and crying: "What do you think of this? Does it work, or should I shred it?"

Plan B: A Poet's Survivors Manual by Sandy McIntosh

University teaching positions have often been the preferred destinations of young American poets. But with the success of MFA programs, when tens of thousands of graduates vie for the limited availability of part-time and full-time teaching posts, many will have to look elsewhere for work. Many will have to devise and follow a Plan B. The award-winning poet, Sandy McIntosh, having lost an early teaching assignment, launched a life-long career in projects that utilized his writing abilities. Instead of corrupting his poetry, he shows how working in different writing genres enhances personal creative work, at the same time it provides a financial basis upon which to continue building one's craft.

Craft: A Memoir by Tony Trigilio

An exploration of the writer's craft through a series of short, linked personal essays. Each chapter features an anecdote from the author's development as a writer that illustrates craft elements central to his body of work. *Craft: A Memoir* is an effort to understand craft through discussions of the direct experience of writing itself—through stories of how Trigilio became a writer. When we talk about "craft" as writers, we frequently focus on clinical, literary-dictionary terms such as language, narrative, structure, image, tone, and voice, among others. To be sure, this book considers such conventional craft elements—especially questions of language, narrative, and structure—but as a book focused on storytelling and memoir, it also emphasizes craft elements such as: generative strategies and revision; persona and voicing; appropriation and remixing; documentary poetics; traditional and experimental poetic forms (including the role that an expanded conception of "ekphrasis" can play for twenty-first century writers); the relationship between music composition and poetry; the role of narrative in lyric poetry; the importance of the ordinary and the mundane; the importance for poets of reading prose; and the artistic benefit of blurring the boundary between history and craft.

Where Did Poetry Come From: Some Early Encounters by Geoffrey O'Brien

A memoir in episodes of some early encounters—with the spoken word, the written word, the sung word—in childhood and adolescence, encounters that suggested different aspects of the mysterious and shapeshifting phenomenon imperfectly represented by the abstract noun "poetry." From nursery rhymes and television theme songs, show tunes and advertising jingles, Classic Comics and Bible verses, to first meetings with the poetry of Stevenson, Poe, Coleridge, Ginsberg, and others, it tracks not final assessments but a description of the unexpected revelations that began to convey how poetry "made its presence known before it had been given a name."

Titles From Marsh Hawk Press

Jane Augustine *Arbor Vitae; Krazy; Night Lights; A Woman's Guide to Mountain Climbing*

Tom Beckett *Dipstick (Diptych)*

Sigman Byrd *Under the Wanderer's Star*

Patricia Carlin: *Original Green; Quantum Jitters; Second Nature*

Claudia Carlson *The Elephant House; My Chocolate Sarcophagus; Pocket Park*

Meredith Cole *Miniatures*

Jon Curley *Hybrid Moments; Scorch Marks*

Neil de la Flor *Almost Dorothy; An Elephant's Memory of Blizzards*

Chard deNiord *Sharp Golden Thorn*

Sharon Dolin *Serious Pink*

Steve Fellner *Blind Date with Cavafy; The Weary World Rejoices*

Thomas Fink *Selected Poems & Poetic Series; Joyride; Peace Conference; Clarity and Other Poems; After Taxes; Gossip*

Thomas Fink and Maya D. Mason *A Pageant for Every Addiction*

Norman Finkelstein *Inside the Ghost Factory; Passing Over*

Edward Foster *A Looking-Glass for Traytors; The Beginning of Sorrows; Dire Straits; Mahrem: Things Men Should Do for Men; Sewing the Wind; What He Ought to Know*

Paolo Javier *The Feeling is Actual*

Burt Kimmelman *Abandoned Angel; Somehow*

Burt Kimmelman and Fred Caruso *The Pond at Cape May Point*

Basil King *Disparate Beasts: Basil King's Beastiary, Part Two; 77 Beasts; Disparate Beasts; Mirage; The Spoken Word/The Painted Hand from Learning to Draw/A History*

Martha King *Imperfect Fit*

Phillip Lopate *At the End of the Day: Selected Poems and An Introductory Essay*

Mary Mackey *Breaking the Fever; The Jaguars That Prowl Our Dreams; Sugar Zone; Travelers With No Ticket Home*

Jason McCall *Dear Hero,*

Sandy McIntosh *The After-Death History of My Mother; Between Earth and Sky; Cemetery Chess; Ernesta, in the Style of the Flamenco; Forty-Nine Guaranteed Ways to Escape Death; A Hole In the Ocean; Lesser Lights; Obsessional*

Stephen Paul Miller *Any Lie You Tell Will Be the Truth; The Bee Flies in May; Fort Dad; Skinny Eighth Avenue; There's Only One God and You're Not It*

Daniel Morris *Blue Poles; Bryce Passage;*

Hit Play; If Not for the Courage

Gail Newman *Blood Memory*

Geoffrey O'Brien *Where Did Poetry Come From; The Blue Hill*

Sharon Olinka *The Good City*

Christina Olivares *No Map of the Earth Includes Stars*

Justin Petropoulos *Eminent Domain*

Paul Pines *Charlotte Songs; Divine Madness; Gathering Sparks; Last Call at the Tin Palace*

Jacquelyn Pope *Watermark*

George Quasha *Things Done for Themselves*

Karin Randolph *Either She Was*

Rochelle Ratner *Balancing Acts; Ben Casey Days; House and Home*

Michael Rerick *In Ways Impossible to Fold*

Corrine Robins *Facing It; One Thousand Years; Today's Menu*

Eileen R. Tabios *The Connoisseur of Alleys; I Take Thee, English, for My Beloved; The In(ter)vention of the Hay(na)ku; The Light Sang as It Left Your Eyes; Reproductions of Empty Flagpole; Sun Stigmata; The Thorn Rosary*

Eileen R. Tabios and j/j hastain *The Relational Elations of Orphaned Algebra*

Susan Terris *Familiar Tense; Ghost of Yesterday; Natural Defenses*

Lynne Thompson *Fretwork*

Madeline Tiger *Birds of Sorrow and Joy*

Tana Jean Welch *Latest Volcano*

Harriet Zinnes: *Drawing on the Wall; Light Light or the Curvature of the Earth; New and Selected Poems; Weather is Whether; Whither Nonstopping*

Tony Trigilio: *Proof Something Happened*

YEAR	AUTHOR	TITLE	JUDGE
2004	Jacquelyn Pope	*Watermark*	Marie Ponsot
2005	Sigman Byrd	*Under the Wanderer's Star*	Gerald Stern
2006	Steve Fellner	*Blind Date with Cavafy*	Denise Duhamel
2007	Karin Randolph	*Either She Was*	David Shapiro
2008	Michael Rerick	*In Ways Impossible to Fold*	Thylias Moss
2009	Neil de la Flor	*Almost Dorothy*	Forrest Gander
2010	Justin Petropoulos	*Eminent Domain*	Anne Waldman
2011	Meredith Cole	*Miniatures*	Alicia Ostriker
2012	Jason McCall	*Dear Hero,*	Cornelius Eady
2013	Tom Beckett	*Dipstick (Diptych)*	Charles Bernstein
2014	Christina Olivares	*No Map of the Earth Includes Stars*	Brenda Hillman
2015	Tana Jean Welch	*Latest Volcano*	Stephanie Strickland
2016	Robert Gibb	*After*	Mark Doty
2017	Geoffrey O'Brien	*The Blue Hill*	Meena Alexander
2018	Lynne Thompson	*Fretwork*	Jane Hirshfield
2019	Gail Newman	*Blood Memory*	Marge Piercy
2020	Tony Trigilio	*Proof Something Happened*	Susan Howe

ARTISTIC ADVISORY BOARD

Toi Derricotte, Denise Duhamel, Marilyn Hacker, Allan Kornblum (in memorium), Maria Mazzioti Gillan, Alicia Ostriker, Marie Ponsot (in memorium), David Shapiro, Nathaniel Tarn, Anne Waldman, and John Yau. For more information, please go to: www.marshhawkpress.org